Born in 1944, Polly Devlin is a well-known broadcaster and journalist who has worked in both Britain and America. She is the author of *The Vogue Book of Fashion Photography* and is a regular contributor to many magazines and newspapers including the *Sunday Times*.

All of us There
POLLY DEVLIN

THE
BLACKSTAFF
PRESS

BELFAST

First published in 1983 by George Weidenfeld and Nicolson Limited
Published by Pan Books Limited in 1984, with its Pavanne edition
published in 1988

This Blackstaff Press edition is a photolithographic facsimile of
the Pavanne edition, printed by Richard Clay Limited, Bungay, Suffolk

This paperback edition published in 1994 by
The Blackstaff Press Limited
3 Galway Park, Dundonald, Belfast BT16 0AN, Northern Ireland

Printed by The Guernsey Press Company Limited

A catalogue record for this book is available from the British Library

ISBN 0-85640-532-9

Grateful acknowledgement is made for permission to reprint extracts from the
following copyright books: *Langrishe Go Down* by Aidan Hiddins (Calder &
Boyars); *The Land of England* by Dorothy Hartley (Macdonald & Janes Pub.
Ltd); *Long Shadows Cast Before* by C. E. B. Brett (John Bartholomew & Son
Ltd); *Who Do You Think You Are?* by Oliver Gillie (Hart-Davis MacGibbon);
'Addlestrop' by Edward Thomas from *The Collected Poems of Edward Thomas*,
edited by R. George Thomas, 1978 (Oxford University Press); 'Sunlight' by
Seamus Heaney from *North*, 'Wedding Day' by Seamus Heaney from *Wintering
Out*, 'Personal Helicon' by Seamus Heaney from *Death of a Naturalist* (Faber &
Faber Ltd). The statistics on Northern Ireland in chapter 15 have been taken
from *Ulster* by the *Sunday Times* Insight Team (Penguin, 1972).

To my brother
Barry Paul Devlin

ACKNOWLEDGEMENTS I am deeply indebted to many people for their help and encouragement during the writing of this book; to Sheila Murphy, who encouraged me from the beginning; to Alex MacCormick, my editor; to Sue Channing, who tirelessly typed and retyped; to Lynda Frost; to Helen Harvey for her generous help; to Deirdre McSharry; to Paddy Duffy of Coalisland; to Wendy Stevenson for her practical support. I owe an old debt of gratitude to May and Maurice Whitten, to Eileen McKeown, and to Sarah Lappin.

I am especially indebted to Seamus Heaney, not only for the many incomparable lines quoted in the book, but also for the words of the title, which since I first read them in *The Seed Cutter* have worked their stealth.

But most of all I wish to thank my parents, my sisters and my brother, and all those people in Ardboe with whom and among whom I grew up.

Polly Devlin

Now, to pry into roots, to finger slime,
To stare big-eyed Narcissus, into some spring
Is beneath all adult dignity. I rhyme
To see myself, to set the darkness echoing.

'Personal Helicon', Seamus Heaney

1

Here is a photograph held in my imagination, looped in my memory. It exists in seven different versions, in seven different imaginations, but this is how I see it. Seven small children stand captured in the photograph in a descending row, each large-eyed child looking anxiously at the camera with expressions that are appealing, appeasing and eager.

There are six girls and one boy in the photograph, my five sisters, my brother and myself, locked in our descending hierarchy, ensnared in family, caught in place by the lens of a box camera. It is any time in the early 1950s. The ivy which stirred over a half-glimpsed door as the photographer crouched under his black blanket is frozen in the moment. Behind the little group looms an ancient Celtic cross. Around lies a graveyard and water, sky and distance.

The photograph is faded. It is over thirty years old and already has that sepia look which gives old photographs an authenticity, a grandeur and a paradoxical reality missing in newer prints. The sepia acts, for me, as does a wreath on a head: a crown, or a symbol of desolation.

These young faces are stained with something else, in another of time's tricks – or double exposure of the imagination. A look of travail seeps out from under those placatory expressions. The bodies of the children held there for ever in their old poses are alert, as though something within them is perpetually poised for flight. I look down on the image as it floats below the surface of my mind. Each figure glimmers more clearly as I pull the complete image gently to the surface. I am fearful of disturbing them as they have always disturbed me, and as I try to hook them up and out of the slipstream of memory into life, and into my life, I see that their childishness is accentuated by that old and premonitory look on their faces, as though they had perceived already what the world had in store. I look away, disturbed by their haunting fugacity, but they do not go away. They can never go away. I am never free of them.

There are seven children – six sisters and a brother, Elizabeth, Eiram, Siobhain, Morgan, Sinclare, Nell and Barry Paul, the only boy, all bound together by what I thought in those early days was the monumental accident of parenthood, which gave us the same father and laid us in the same womb and endowed me at least with an early, inaccurate and somewhat resentful belief that by the merest stumble of time any one of us could have been the other . . . except for our brother, for he remains perforce outside the family estate of sisterhood, aware of our strange exact connections, deeply affected by them and their repercussions but removed from them by his maleness.

Our births span twelve years, yet we seem always to be seven, forged into each other like crystals on quartz, connected by our name, roots, place, our history, as well as by the knotted, clotted tie of blood. Perhaps most obvious of all, we are connected by our distinctive and characteristic family looks.

Anyone who sees one of those children has seen something of us all; and even as children, uninterested in individual appearance, we recognize that our collective appearance is remarkable. The far set of our big and somewhat prominent eyes, the wide horizontal planes of our faces, the high broad foreheads, the mix of passion and sullenness in the expression, the set of our heads on the shoulders, all are living illustrations of kinship, and throughout childhood there reverberates the cry, 'Isn't the wan like the other?' or, in a phrase that we feel to be somewhat ill-chosen, 'Isn't she the dead spit of her sister?'

For years I find it necessary to believe that our appearance and looks come directly from our father's side – the strong male side, the side with power. But in other photographs – which I refuse to examine while a child and can only now look at without the squint of resentment and remorse with which for so long I distorted them – show that we have inherited as much of our cast of feature from our mother's side as from that of our father; and it took me years to recognize that power was compressed in her like an unfired bullet.

Everyone we meet in our small world, a remote and backward corner of Northern Ireland, knows us 'on' our parents; but since *they* are distinctive in every way we don't feel it is any great feat of recognition, although at a certain level we feel vaguely flattered at our provenance being so known. But we are not at all sure about who we are when we look in the mirror or look right or left and see the sister, that someone else, the separate person who is inseparable from you, the sister who speaks and moves and looks like oneself, and yet is entirely different.

We know that the recognition we are given is not as individuals, but as appurtenances of our parents, and as young members of an old family. Our father is well-known in this enclosed district – first, also, as a child of his parents, the son of a man who vaulted away from his prescribed future and in so doing gave himself just enough status to leave himself isolated, and who married the first school-mistress in the first public elementary school to be established in the district. My father is known as himself too, the owner of the only public house in the district, as an athlete – he was a fine footballer and the county high-jump champion before his marriage – and for his memorably good looks.

My father, like my grandfather, married a school-mistress and she, like her mother-in-law, is from another part of Ireland, which makes her an outsider and compounds her apartness from the community. She is distinctive because of her occupation, because she drives a car – no other woman in the district does, not just because there are few other cars – and because she is blonde of hair and golden of skin, rare colouring in our Celtic district. She met my father soon after she arrived to take up her first teaching job in a tiny school in the adjoining parish of King's Island. They were married within a year, and she found herself transplanted from the carefully structured existence of her middle-class family in Warrenpoint, a pretty seaside town bound by the rigid modes and mores of provincial gentility, into the ramshackle, almost mediaeval, undiluted life of our district with its own distinctive bonding, tribal mores and manners.

What happened to our immediate forbears and affected us profoundly is what usually happens only to people who have left their native place of birth, and met and married someone from different stock and background. Each partner then acquires the preoccupations, priorities, memories, the new ways of family of the other. In the pooling of these they make for themselves in the

11

new place a new life, fuelled by a new energy, and thus give themselves a different future. But the making of the new blood-line and that different future has been accompanied by the febrile, disruptive shock of leaving home, of pulling up old roots.

This breakdown of tribal associations, of personal family history in a particular territory, the loss of lore and legend associated with each family's background, the sunderance of people from place, has never happened to us, nor to anyone who lives where we live. In this place history and life are utterly mingled, and history is alive, bitterly alive, because we live where history happened. Our grandfather and father have married women of different stock, background and religion, but what made them unusual is that they remained where they were, rooted in the same place. The new branches became grafted on to the reckless and sly character-istics of the fisherman stock, and the roots fattened in the soil without having been disturbed.

But something else was disturbing those roots. By the time we arrived the twentieth century, almost half its span late, had arrived too and was encircling our community, about to invade it, weapons and barter goods at the ready: trinkets for the natives, electricity, wireless and television and, most dazzling of all, Social Security. We grew up in that moment between the death throes of the oldest kind of social security and the beginnings of a new dispensa-tion, living in a left-over place operating on a time-scale of its own, with a way of life that still clung softly to the earth, nourishing it and being nourished by it like the fleece on a sheep.

When fleece is cut from the sheep and collected at nightfall, the fleeces are still live and warm. If the summer night is cold after a hot day, a mist like the haze on the Lough clouds the wool and the cooling fleeces stir slightly all night through. In an old wool-room you could hear the fleeces stirring – a faint sound like soft breathing. Our generation in Ardboe were like fleeces cut from the last of the flock.

The place called Ardboe is the most remote region of a remote county – Tyrone – a large rambling shrub- and bush-covered county that stretches across the interior of the political state of Northern Ireland, often called Ulster – a misnomer, since Ulster, one of the four provinces of Ireland, far outreaches the latter-day political boundaries of Northern Ireland. Ardboe is a parish of small townlands, many of whose names are Gaelic. The parish is divided into Upper and Lower Ardboe, the one separated from the other by the enormous wedge of an aerodrome built in the middle of the Second World War, and which landed, all unbeknownst, in the lap of the parish like a monstrous cuckoo.

Lower Ardboe lies along the shores of Lough Neagh, the biggest lake in the United Kingdom, twenty-five miles long by eight miles wide, in effect an inland tideless freshwater sea, an extravagant expanse of water which laps the small fields of our farm, within sight and sound of our house. Its soughing music forms the aural background to each day of our lives.

We are almost an island, connected to the outside world by only one tiny road which dribbles its slack and twisting way into our hidden desmesnes, and which swerves and slings around the perimeter of the aerodrome like a girdle. To anyone coming towards us for the first time from the small market town of Cookstown ten miles away, following the road as it meanders towards the lough, it must appear to expire in a flaxhole and a tangle of bramble below the Moor Hill. But in fact, at that point, called the Cross Roads (although it is not strictly that), it turns at a right-angle, narrows and plunges towards Biddy's Brae, past our house and thence to the Old Cross of Ardboe, where it ends in the graveyard surrounding the Cross. Another smaller spur road called the Car Road branches off alongside the lough shore towards the flat long beauty of Golloman's Point, and parallel to that old turf road is a new white concrete road leading to the pump house built for a water-supply to the aerodrome. Both these roads are hidden from view on the road to the Cross.

That road links us to our landscape in the same way that our sisterhood links us together. It is an absolute connection and has the quality of infinity as it stretches ahead in a green and blue haze. Along its way old men and sometimes an old woman lean over their gates or against a sagging gate-post made from the branch of a tree, waiting with an endless curiosity for our approach, as though they had never ever seen us before, nor even the likes of us, though they have known us from babyhood. They like to vex us with questions as to our goodness and badness, and

13

what book we are in at school. In their day, when public elementary schooling was first established, each grade of pupil was reckoned according to which textbook she or he had attained and the form still lingers. We were always wary of the questioners and their questions and indeed they were asked to vex us, rather than from genuine interest, and sometimes adults did things that left us feeling helplessly violated; we were never sure why or when and thus we tended to be on guard.

'Do you remember Carrie's Joe?' Eiram once asked me. 'He always sat over by the yew tree in the graveyard.'

He'd have been married to Kitty who had sometimes helped Ellen look after us older children when a new baby arrived. No one according to our legend – springing, as did all our legends, from our father – had liked Carrie's Joe or his brother John, least of all their wives. When he died Kitty (whatever she may have inwardly felt) outwardly lamented and grieved. 'He's gone', she said wildly to Maggie her sister-in-law, 'and left me on me lone.' Maggie looked at her with narrowed envious eyes. 'I wish I had your story to tell,' she said.

I reminded Eiram of the story. 'He did something horrible to me', Eiram said, 'something traumatic. I was down in their house and I was wearing a white fur coat, a teddy-bear coat, that came in that parcel from America. You often wore it too. I was about five or six, I suppose, and some of the family were cutting wood in the kitchen, putting it under the range, and I was bending down helping them. Carrie's Joe was sitting on the settle smoking his pipe and I suddenly saw him clearing his throat and spitting on to my coat, and I thought that it couldn't be true, that it must be an accident. I was so embarrassed and ashamed, I didn't know what to do. And Kitty, his wife, saw him and shouted, "You old brute. You bad, dirty old brute. Ruining the child's coat," and she took me out of the house. She knew, too, that he'd meant it. But the smell of that spit and smoke. My hatred of smoking isn't accidental.'

'But why did they do things like that, Eiram?' I asked.

'It was jealousy in an odd sort of way,' she replied. 'I remember someone once saying that it was the pastime of men to torment the children. Don't you remember how, coming home from

14

school, we always dreaded meeting men? Because we never knew how they would react?'

I did not. I remember the odd men and old men who were occupied with more mysterious things than we could comprehend, as well as men who always seemed utterly preoccupied in their own pursuits, cycling to and from their fishing on the lough, or leading horses, or driving a cow to be serviced by our bull, or wielding a great curved billhook to the thorn hedges, ploughing the fields alongside the road, or spraying the potato plants from a copper tank strapped to their backs. I always marvelled at how radically the looks of all of the fields – except the Fallow Field – were changed by the cycle of their crops.

The potato and flax fields were particularly dramatic. In the spring the potato fields were a mass of green foliage and white flowers, rich and dense, which became a rich speckled blue, the colour of thrushes' eggs, after the plants had been sprayed with the blue stone and soda mix to protect them from the blight, the cause of the famine that is as much a watershed in Irish history as the Great War is in English history. In the late autumn, when the potatoes had been gathered and schools were closed so that we could help with the picking, the bare brown fields were studded with storage pits which looked like burial mounds.

Flax was a beautiful crop and its feathery growth had, from any distance, a limpid greenness that moved fluently in the slightest wind and became the background to a marvellous blueness when it flowered. There were few flowers to be seen in our district of tiny farms and no gardens, where all vegetation was green sprinkled with white or pink blossom on the bramble and thorn and wild fruit trees; and these sudden rich bluenesses seemed extraordinary in that landscape, exotic and unnatural. The flax had to be pulled out by hand, since it grew mingled with thistle and weed, so harvesting it was a painful and back-breaking business. After it was pulled, it was put to soak in the flaxholes that lay festering and stagnant in the corners of low-lying fields, surrounded by the heavy stones which held it under water. When the flax had rotted – or retted – in the holes for a month or more it was lifted out, slimy and foetid, and was spread on smooth pasture to dry, and its strange, sour stench hung across the countryside. You could almost see that smell, vaporizing and shimmering acidly over the fields.

The word flaxen has lost – or has never had – its scorch and meaning for anyone who has not seen that lovely metamorphosis from a green plant to a glimmering strand, a silky blondeness, so shimmering with light that it seemed on the point of igniting into incandescence. It did ignite often, because of its extreme dryness, and the flax mill in Upper Ardboe went up in flames with defeating regularity and all the work and crop went with it, lost. 'You could be sure', my father said, 'if you saw a pall of smoke over by Oiney's Michael's in Mullinahoe that the flax mill was on fire again.'

He said it with great restraint, considering that when it burnt down he had generally lost his crop. Every part of the process of making linen out of flax was tedious and fraught, and even, in the system of scutching – the crushing of the fibres by rolling and beating – dangerous, since they had to be held in the hand against spindles rotating at high speed; many a man lost more than a crop. When the linen was woven it was pale brown, or greyish-brown, not white at all, and it was stretched out on smooth pasture to be bleached by the sun and the weather.

The best flax field in our district was at the Moor Hill, where a fairy tree grew, near Rosy Campbell's house. We always had an uneasy feeling passing this house which we attributed, if we tried to reason it out at all, to the presence of the fairy tree and its omens. Certainly the atmosphere of unease there had to do with powerful superstition – but not wholly. There was a rational explanation, although as children we did not know it and breathed in the air of unease and insecurity as a natural part of things. The land bailiff had lived in that house; for even such an obscure and poverty-stricken parish as Ardboe had been part of a great estate given to an English family – the Alexanders – who lived in a Great House some thirty miles distant, and who collected rents and dues until the land was ceded back to the descendants of the earlier dispossessed. If there had been a bad season, or a remittance payment from an emigrant son or daughter did not come through and the rent was defaulted on, a farmer might lose his cow, or his crop, or worst of all be evicted in lieu of payment. Though those days had gone when we hurried past the Campbell house, the insecurity and threat still lingered around it.

2

The seven of us were born during and after the Second World War and, although cameras were scarce and film almost unobtainable, our family archaeology lies in photographs, rare visual relics. Every one, however faded and amateur in composition, holds a detonating charge that shifts my heart, partly because of the *lacrimae rerum* through which it seems I must look at them, and also because to my eyes the children in them each bear a look of bruised innocence, of anxious love, both somehow emphasized by the openness and width of the faces, and by the expressions glazed over them like the thinnest of icings. These expressions can only be described as being the utter opposite of street-wise – here is a disturbed simplicity, a signalling of goodwill and trust.

Perhaps all old photographs of the person one has been and the people one has known in early life bear this look of innocence; the faces lack the engraved mark of time which has so slowly but irrevocably altered the face that looks down on its own youth. The image below one's now-knowing eyes lies waiting to accommodate the experience borne on the face above, which has been arrived at at a cost that might seem too high if it were known in advance. I remember reading once of how mushrooms had, over four hundred years, raised a huge flagstone with their subtle and stubborn growth; looking at ourselves in these photographs, time seems like that – silently pressing on to that young skin with a terrible, tiny power until suddenly it has arrived whole and I am here, now, as I am.

Mixed with this innocence is a wariness and a look, common to all, of anxiety – and though the photographs give only surface clues to what goes on underneath, I know that anxiety lies at our centre, and unspecified guilt, a legacy of the hurry of sisters and of our religious upbringing, and inherited too from our father, and from our mother. Her inclination to sadness and panic was diverted into practicality and endemic anxiety, as counterpoint and balance to her husband's nature; he embraced melancholy with a voluptuous sentimentality.

The photographs are a mixed lot, some stuck arbitrarily without any real chronology into old home-made, ribbon-bound books and some that, paradoxically, although they seem the most familiar (in that they are so much a part of the formal, fixed scenery of the household that for a long time I never really examine them), show us in our most unfamiliar aspects. They look more like icons than family likenesses. These are the formal studies taken by a professional photographer in his studio in Belfast and they appear to me to have less to do with us as we are, or were, than with my mother's brave attempts to lead and to have us lead a more normal life than she can ever really have in the place to which marriage has transported her. There she leads an eccentric, starved existence, while her whole being and imagination yearn for a proper and conventional life. In these portraits it even appears that our mother has succeeded in her quest to make us into children fit for that living world of her memory and dreams and desires. We lean demurely against the studio pillars and ornate chairs, and stare, grave and neat, from underneath fringes that cover our foreheads or from under enormous ribbons that strain our hair back from our faces so tightly that our foreheads gleam and bulge. Something ravening in us is subdued in those portraits, but there is little real connection between the living creatures and the children in the photographs. We have posed to please in them.

In her lost urban world, left behind so long ago, normal families pose formally for their annual photographs and the resulting portraits stand on pianos or hang on walls. But nothing is formal in our world sunk so deeply into the land; or rather the formality has to do with the reticence of manners and the careful ways of treating with each other as human beings engaged in a struggle for survival rather than for social position.

There is no place in this world for aspirations towards ancestry. In any case our ancestry and that of everyone around lives on in the foundations of our daily lives, and is enshrined in the names of the townlands, the landmarks, the small hillocks – the Moor Hill, Biddy's Brae, the Eglish Rising, in the corners and twists in the single road – Dan Daisy's bend, the kiln corner, Grainne's corner; in the names of the trees – Matty's thorn, the Pig Tree, Treanor's rookery, the Pin Tree. Every field too has its name, crop, characteristic and lore. The Fallow Field has never been ploughed; the Bush Hill has a fairy tree in the middle which is never lopped or disturbed; the Car Road Field lies alongside the old original road that once was the main traverse across the district; and Matty's Hill commemorates an old widower whose tiny cottage has long since gone to earth. Yet we have already begun to slip out of this world, or occupy a slightly ambivalent position within it – partly because of our parents' occupations in a district where everyone else's work is connected with the land or the water, and partly because of that long reach our male forbears made to bring in mates from outside the district and from a different class – the class that finds it demeaning, rather than descriptive, to be called peasants.

Our grandfather – handsome, autocratic, who signed his name John Sinnamond Devlin in a proud copperplate flourish – married a soft-haired Miss Walsh from Waterford, at the other end of Ireland, who had come to teach in the upper parish. A generation before, his father had married a woman from the far side of the lough whom he met when, as a fisherman, he fished the whole of the lough. Such free days are gone by the time we are growing up. No one would dare to venture so far out for fear of the bailiffs who still ruled the water for an absentee landlord.

The woman my grandfather married had a completely different blood-line from his. She was of Scottish Presbyterian descent, big-boned and fair-haired, while his breed was small-boned and Celtic. To this mixture has been added Huguenot blood from my mother's mother. Her maiden name was Cadeau and, when our mother mentions this, the information is received in fairly sullen silence. It is a name that makes no reference to Ardboe and we recognize from an early age that my father cannot abide my mother to talk about her life before they were married or to speak of anything that has happened to her which lies outside his own experience and narrow territories. He is bored and threatened by any embarkation on a subject he finds alien, and this boredom and unease are communicated in a kind of furious, rude impatience which some of us share and guiltily condone. Because we love him so passionately, we must endorse his attitudes. So although one part of our character is interested, indeed avid for her stories of before her marriage, another part is resentful and jealous; we do not want to listen or to recognize that for her a wistful world exists outside our own, where we are physically so firmly lodged in a way of life that, although we cannot know it, is already a historical curiosity and has made misfits of us for the future that awaits.

Whenever our mother speaks of her life in Newry, where she was born, and Warrenpoint, where she was brought up, every nuance in her voice suggests to me – although here I am prospecting through the geology of old guilts, love and resentment rather than memory – that the places of her young girlhood had been golden cities, peopled with glorious heroes, all vanished or banished; and I minded and resented this on her account as well as our own. As a child I felt that all of us by each of our comings had dragged her down to her present existence, in which there were no white-socked, jolly girls and boys with ruddy faces setting out to play tennis or to go swimming in Killowen, or gathering in each other's houses in the evening for sing-songs around the piano, and fast conversation to do with films and the wireless, but instead only a quiverful of demanding dependants, and intellectual loneliness.

She keeps about her an extraordinary innocent quality, a bruised innocence, and even after bearing seven children she still wears the same look that she has in the only photograph we see of her as a child. This is another studio photograph, with the look of a Daguerrotype. The young family in it is beautiful, but their mother's face is hard above the fall of white lace at the neck of her long black dress, which in turn makes a background for the glimmering silky shapes of her three pale children. Our mother stands at the front of the photograph, and May and Maurice, her younger twin sister and brother, lean back, linked within the loose embrace of their mother's arm. Soon after the photograph was

20

taken Maurice died in the influenza epidemic of 1918, which also killed his father. My mother's mother turned to her for comfort; but who, I used to wonder, could comfort a bereaved ten-year-old who had become the stay of a small family?

'We lived on Sugar Island', she said, 'and from the windows of the drawing room, which was on the first floor, you could see everything that was happening.' The glamour of it was heart-stopping, the idea of living in the centre of a town. And the very name was so marvellous. Nothing in Ardboe could match up to it, and when I looked at photographs of my mother and father on the day they were married, leaning over the backs of two deck chairs, laughing in the orchard, I felt that we were the apples already budding in that new paradise as they, hand in hand, with wandering steps and slow through Eden took their solitary way. And I never doubted when I was small but that all my sisters shared my apprehension of their exile. Added to my resentment, my wish for her to be happy, was the sullen self-inflicted pain of blame, the pain that so many children silently bear and which she herself still bore.

The two of them were like parables for their strange country: she straight, fair, often hostile; he pliant, appeasing, charming. She utterly refused to be seduced, fought her corner like a tiger, and for years I hated her for it, and for her refusal to be seduced by us or by the man she had chosen to marry. She eschewed charm; she had witnessed at too close quarters its ruinous effects, had seen what a weapon it was, a way of evading responsibility, a way of deflecting hostility, and the chief resource of many a feckless and reckless man.

Something always seems unmeshed. Many years later, Eiram, the sister whom this book is perhaps most about and who is married to a poet, said: 'Although in one deep way I believe my childhood to have been halcyon, to have been uniquely rich, I felt and sometimes feel deep sorrow in reality and remembrance. Why? Because of the tendencies of human nature? Some inherited genetic strain? Because, after all, our father's side was inclined to melancholia. Perhaps both of those. But it was something more than self-pity that gave us that feeling of flight that made us always mark time there . . .

'Certainly the basis for that premature sense of loss was given to us by our religion and by our parents. Our mother always seemed to be holding fire and, without even being conscious of it herself, she passed that feeling of suspension on to us, that waiting for another better place, somewhere else where life is real. We lived with a feeling that we were really only here on sufferance, that life really would be after this our exile in a valley of tears, and all our prayers certainly reinforced that. So I couldn't believe it when, after I had grown up, I discovered my husband didn't have this sense of loss, this feeling of being left behind. He thinks if a place is empty then he's the first there. That magical ring of confidence, that confidence in yourself and your own senses eluded us, eluded all our family. His family life was utterly together, like an egg contained within the shell, without any quality of otherness, without the sense of loss that this otherness brings. They had confidence in the way they lived, a lovely impeccable confidence in their own style.

Afterwards I read one of his poems, 'North', about his kitchen and the space and presences there, which ended:

. . . and here is love,
Like a tinsmith's scoop,
Sunk past its gleam
In the meal-bin.*

I knew what he was talking about – who could not with such an image – and love was there somewhere in our kitchen, but what was not sunk and was glittering above love was the sharp edge of anxiety.

Caught between the flat mysterious lands of the aerodrome – forbidden and alien territory looming around our doorstep – the dead-end of the graveyard and the vast soughing of the water, we lived in a left-over atavistic world, generations away from the rest of the post-war world of Britain, out of kilter with the chronology of the century. We were like preserved, resurrected relics from an earlier age, characters from a science-fiction story in which everything has been frozen and then rocketed through the slip-

* Seamus Heaney.

stream of time into a thinner, more exhausted future where our present is everywhere else long past. We became enmeshed in our own myth, the secret mythology of sisterhood; and although we did not then know it we were already enmeshed in the larger mythology of Ireland and being Irish, engaged in the strange battle between being natives of a place and yet having no security or power in that place.

The myths, the secrecies, the pulls of history and our strivings to get free of any or all of it were surrounded by the biggest, most pervasive myth of all – our church and our religion. Sometimes as I lay staring through the skylight of our pink hayshed I felt I could see in the cloud-ruptured sky above me another kind of skylight; and through it above me like the rings around Saturn were those magic circles, almost clashing as they enclosed us. It seemed an impossible task to escape them and we knew that no one could come to free us. We had to get ourselves out and at times I felt like Marsyas crying to Apollo as he delicately flayed and peeled his skin: 'Why do you tear me from myself?'

3

While we are small, locked into our time and place, we never consider the possibility that we may one day be separated, although we know, literally in our blood, that we will be and must be. We dread our separation, yearn for it, run away from it, run towards it. Wherever we are, in time, in place, its possibility is there, anticipated, rejected, embraced. We move closer to preempt it, and bear in on each other so hard that when one moves and shifts the rest are affected. We arrange and disarrange (sometimes inadvertently, sometimes venomously) our interlinked present, and compose the patterns for each other's future; and each of us in building, piece on piece, the complicated structures of our own life also builds the scaffolding and the obstacles for each other. The edifices never seem to be finished.

'No man's life is worth anything if it is not an allegory,' wrote Keats, and each of our lives has an allegorical significance for the others. We are all points of reference on the ordnance maps of each other's lives and take our bearings from the various eminences and sloughs not only in our own life but also in the life of each sister. The important spaces that we are constantly, psychically mapping out for ourselves are as thick with each other's meaning and pressures as the actual space we occupy. Every one of us – from Elizabeth, the eldest, who had us all at her heels and was and is the lynch-pin in our lives, to Nell, the youngest, who we surmise often had to cope with the additional burden of feeling bereft – was either pursuing someone or being pursued, or both. It took years for us to find our own pace, to create a silence in which to hear only the sound of our own footsteps and not feel that the silence was a lonely emptiness.

There were every day in our linked world endless opportunities for betrayal, self-betrayal and treachery. These power-struggles, so gargantuan and dynastic to us, were merely irritating squabbles to adult eyes, squabbles about nothing, and there was no use trying to explain that to us they were about everything on earth. Each one of us worked out ways of dealing with our place in the hierarchy with more or less success, and we each played the role of mother, sibling, dependant, enemy or confidante, slipping from one to the other as we looked covertly at the sisters above or below or parallel to us. We locked into interlinked overlapping circles – being older, younger, inferior, superior, big girl, or baby depending on who was treating with whom and how.

The establishment of identity, of separateness and finally of love – for everything in these kind of testaments silts down to love, or the lack of it – was made more difficult by the fact that in this intense, backward world we think we live on a slope down which everything slides to the youngest child, whom everyone, except my parents, called the babby or the ba. The Ba is a totem for affection, the only human being whom adults in our old, repressed, modest and fanatically chaste society can unrestrainedly and unashamedly caress without inhibition. Her apparent helplessness is a powerful weapon, since because she can still cry with a monstrous innocence, assurance, spontaneity and, of course, considerable volume, she receives the most of anything that may be available in the way of adult attention. And since each new sister arrives before the previous, emotionally insatiable child has received enough protection, love and attention to proceed securely alone, there is, we believe, inserted at our core a particle of anxiety that grows with our growth and becomes as fat, cherished and unnecessary as a pearl. We know that if we mustered up the nerve to emulate that lusty solipsistic noise we would speedily get what Ellen, our young housekeeper and maid of all work, calls a 'quare clipe' on the ear.

We are all experts at suffering vicariously, especially if the pain is inflicted by someone outside our family ring (Ellen is an essential link in it). When one sister is threatened or alarmed, or when some ominous event looms, it is as though an invisible thread between our bodies has suddenly tautened, and the others are drawn towards the source of the twitching disturbance. Any outside threat possesses an unknowable, arbitrary, swooping quality and we are constantly on guard against it, since any attack on one of us constitutes an attack on us all, any breach in our circle renders each one more vulnerable. We always know, even when apart, when any one of us is in trouble. A reprimand, a slap, any kind of verbal or physical assault on one from a teacher or any adult other than a parent or Ellen makes the others alert. We converge towards our punished sister from wherever we are scattered.

Naturally enough, our figures of authority dislike this collective empathic response and interpret it as recalcitrance or defiance, both of which are labelled 'boldness'. Being labelled 'a bold girl' is fierce criticism; but our response is hardly bold. Most of our misdeeds are inadvertent rather than calculated and we are placatory, initially or superficially. But lying very close under that timid surface is a spirit ready to let fly at any encroachment that suddenly goes too far.

Although we unite and close ranks against any outside threats and dangers, each sister remains the beloved enemy, the 'smyler with the knyfe under her cloyke'. But this kind of danger from

25

within, although aggressive, is not alarming, since it is part of our scheme of things and lies within our gift and understanding. That instinctive response to outsiders is an integral part of our sisterhood; and it is to try to loosen those familial psychic knots that link us so tightly together that we simultaneously insist so fiercely on our separateness and individuality, our independence, and our place in the hierarchy of the family.

Elizabeth was, as all first-borns must be, both a pioneer and a link between us and our parents, as well as the first link in the ring of children. She bore considerable stress; she tempered herself to it. In the earliest of the family photographs she is being held aloft proudly by her dashing and beautiful father. They both pose without guile; she in his arms as though in the branches of a tree, taking his surrounding strength and adulation for granted and, perhaps, for security; she looks carefree. But in later photographs she has lost that carefree look, that creamy candour, although her face becomes more beautiful, with eyes like huge green globes, such lustrous eyes, rimmed by thick, slightly sticky eyelashes, and her hair a mix of chestnut and the darkest chocolate brown. She looks more Spanish than Irish, as compact, burnished and contained as the conker from a horse-chestnut newly taken from its round and spiky cell.

Eiram, born two years later, looked like a true Celt with her thin skin and fine features, her shining hair high-lighted with red gleams and her frisky, athletic body that always seemed so much more in control of itself than I can ever make mine be. No matter how hard I push my body – and it always seems completely separate from me – it refuses to respond in the way that Eiram's seems to respond, so faultlessly and effortlessly. Her flesh, muscles and bones seem compact, vividly integrated, whereas I feel my flesh as something vulnerable, cumbrous, laid loose over my bones.

Eiram looms all over life. I think of her constantly. It seems to me an extraordinary and dreadful imbalance that if I had not been born she would have been living a life without me, unknowingly devoid, and yet without her existence as the second child, I, the third, could never have been. It took me years to recognize the profound effect which my birth had on her, only a baby of fourteen months when I was born; looking back, it seems as though I was determined to catch up on her from the moment I became aware of her out there ahead. The pressure on both of us was inevitable.

From an early age I became taller than Eiram and although I do not look Celtic at all, I think I could only be Irish. And these physical patterns are almost exactly repeated in the next three children. This relationship of appearance and characteristics to rank of birth used to make me marvel, for I thought then that my rank of birth was mere chance, that I might easily have been older than Eiram and indeed that the slightest falter in time's slippery arrangements might have transposed any one of us into being the other. Only later, reading the work of Karl König, the psychologist and educator who made a study of the special characteristics of brothers and sisters and believed that there are no more than the four fundamental types of children – the only child, the first-born, the second and the third – did I find that my marvelling was a basis for research. He believed, too, that if there are more than three children in a family then the fundamental features of the first three are repeated, and that the rank of birth in the family constellation imprints traits upon each one of us; that the order of birth is of the deepest significance and influence in our destiny, and that the particular rank moulds the habits of the bearer. The facts, as ever with such speculations, fit the philosophy.

Elizabeth and Eiram seemed to me to be bonded together in a miraculous and lovely ring that was beyond my reach or power or penetration. They had established these bonds before my birth, but I resented them as though they had been maliciously premeditated, forged merely to spite me, and I longed to join hands in their magic circle; but magic circles cannot expand or open without some kind of charm and I had no spells to cast, no charms, nothing valuable to offer, to bribe or buy my way. So I loved them and hated them and wished that ill might befall them so that they would need me to rescue them. Most of all I wanted them to want me, and make my existence, so apparently superfluous, into something necessary and worthy. It was an impossible, mute want, literally unspeakable, since children cannot perceive these patterns. They cannot ask for what they do not know they want.

'I believe', Eiram said years later, 'that our unhappiness in childhood – if one thinks it was unhappy, and I don't – had far more to do with the sisterly mafia above and around us than it had to do with parents. I was very close to Elizabeth and your not being of it made my relationship with her more exclusive and precious. We didn't do it deliberately or malevolently, although I knew at the time you wanted to be with us. I was hostile to you because I felt threatened by you. It seemed to me that there was a definite hierarchy in the house: parents first, Elizabeth afterwards, me next, then you. But you absolutely refused to accept that hierarchy without a struggle, you would never accept your place, and I could never be sure you wouldn't preempt my position, take what was mine by right – and you tried to every time, at every opportunity. You fought your corner day in and day out.'

These erupting moments of physical combat, although comparatively rare, always seem imminent. At such times nothing exists except the rage and pain and bodily strength of the sister-enemy. It is like love-making in reverse and shakes the whole house; we never do it when our parents are around and Ellen knows the only way of breaking us apart is to send or threaten to send for our father. 'Away out quick, quick, you', she screams at whatever sister has not been speedy enough to disappear, 'and get the boss before the pair of them has each other kilt. Oh Jaysus, they'll not leave gutties of each other.'

Whoever is sent to fetch our father goes with a heavy heart and foreboding, for we hate invoking him – he is omnipotent and none of us wish to bear the weight of this omnipotence. Telling him of our quarrels or letting him see us in anger is one of our taboos – we must always disguise our passion and anger from him, partly because we feel he cannot accommodate it; it is too distressing for him, who is, for us, the epitome of love. His love is something apart from the rest of the loves in our life, the complex bitter love we feel for the women-sisters, mothers, keepers – who populate our lives. He is our maypole, the centre of our chanting circle,

28

around which we dance. Our love for him is so filled with magic, so much a thing of spells and air, that our love for and the love of the women around us, love that might redeem us, seems in comparison so ordinary, so commonplace, so abrupt, so unspoken, so hedged about with busyness, anxiety and grudgery, so entangled with dismay, grievance and jealousy that we can only perceive it as a thing of duty and grudgery, a substitute.

We danced around our father, small Salomes, and believed fiercely, passionately that he was the only pivot of that ring, that he was the source of strength and the spring of power. We could not admit what we knew at some profound level to be the truth – that our mother was the stronger. It was inadmissible that a woman should be stronger. It would have shocked us to admit it, so we refused the knowledge and made a guard ring around him. We kept our eyes fixed on the Man and pushed away the other incompatible knowledge of mad bad female strength, by its nature wicked, unclean, immodest, unchaste and worst of all unnatural. We danced and circled and formed a ring, thinking it was a dance of obedience and enchantment, when it was a war-dance, full of fear, and we were snarling with protectiveness against the enemy without. If we had been able to look away from that central figure we would have seen that the enemy we were keeping at bay was our mother; and that she was in there, with him, all the time.

This attitude subsisted in the society around us; our obeisances to our male were repeated at every level. Women reared their girl children as they themselves were reared, to defer to the males in their family, to give them the best seats, to dance attendance, to try to anticipate every wish. These attitudes made enemies of men and women, and they might have spoken different languages for all the communication that seemed to take place between the sexes – it was always more in the manner of a negotiation than a communication, and even as a child there was always the feeling that, when one was playing with a boy, one was a collaborator rather than a friend.

In the adult world around us men and women had little social life together. Even married couples seemed to live separate lives and their married night-life was more often than not conducted in a bed in a room shared with the rest of the family. Young

29

couples, of whom there were few, shared what they could in whatever space they could find – under a hedge or down by a shed – and could be denounced from the pulpit for so doing.

Many men – fathers, sons, grandfathers – spent their evenings in the local pub, which women never entered. On Sundays at Mass the men and boys gathered outside the church walls to talk, and the younger men bashfully to watch the young women hurry into the church. Inside, the congregation was completely segregated with men on the right, women on the left; and after Mass the women hurried home, while some of the men stayed to toss pennies or drink an illicit stout in a shuttered back-room, or to walk home at a more leisurely pace to the dinner the women were already cooking. The legacy of such divides seemed to be a feeling of contempt on both sides, and suspicion, distrust and a certain amount of fear – of men for women and *vice versa* – fear of the unknown, if of nothing else.

The small and alarming society of my sisters is in some ways a simulacrum of that world ahead of us; and in another is utterly removed from any resemblance to the real thing – perhaps all childhood worlds are – but the imbalance in ratio of male and female in the family and the way that males were treated gave any male who entered our perception an overwhelming importance which it has been very hard to alter.

'What's talla, Daddy?' Nell said to my father one evening. She was three.

'What's what?'

'Talla.'

Ellen began to make horrific signals and faces at Nell behind Daddy's back, but Nell took no notice.

'Tallow,' he said. 'Tallow is the stuff that candles are made out of. Wherever did you get that from?'

'I didn't get it', Nell said, 'but Joe-Pat MacAllister's going to beat it out of Francey.'

Daddy laughed and Ellen went into the scullery, painted with a pink distemper that peeled off in friable patches leaving a mottled blue underneath. I ate these patches, as though compelled by some biological instinct rather than taste or hunger, if in search of some vital ingredient, and when the wall came to be more blue than pink Ellen began to watch out for who was doing it, and pounced as I surreptitiously slipped a lump between my lips.

'Oh, Holy Jaysus', she said, 'and Father, Son, would you look at what she's doing. You'll not be happy till you have the house down round us.'

Now I followed her to try to find the meaning of the signals. 'What's wrong?' I whispered. 'What were you looking at Nell like that for?'

Ellen looked at me consideringly. 'Because I thought she was going to tell the boss that I said I would beat the talla out of her,' Ellen said. 'You couldn't be up to what she'd say. She could spay fortunes, that one.'

'Did you say you'd beat the talla out of her?' I asked.

'I did,' Ellen said, 'for she knocked over a pot of water on my good clean floor I had only washed and I'd warned her fornenst it. When did Joe-Pat MacAllister say he would beat it out of Francey and for why?'

'Because he was playing,' I said, and there was more truth to it than I knew.

None of the MacAllisters seem frightened of anything apart from Joe-Pat, their father. He married Maisie, his cousin, in the same year as my father and mother were married, and one or other of the two women seems always to be pregnant or just to have had a child, the dreaded ba. The MacAllisters live even nearer the lough than we do, in a two-roomed, tin-roofed cottage. We are friends because of the proximity of our families and our ages, rather than because of any great warmth or attraction between us; indeed the friendship is shaky and wary on our side since there is a streak of cruelty bordering on the sadistic in the older MacAllister boys, which is not surprising when we think of how they are treated at home. Their father is often violent, his eyes wild in his face, and he seems, as did many Irish parents of that generation, to equate the sound of children laughing with being bad. The MacAllister children suffer real physical pain daily, yet they seem to accommodate it in a more successful way than we seem to accommodate our emotional pain. The effects emerge later.

My mother once tentatively tried to intercede on the MacAllister children's behalf in her capacity as school-teacher and mentor, rather than as another parent (for that would have caused great offence), by suggesting to Joe-Pat that it might be worth beating his children less and encouraging them more; but Joe-Pat explained patiently, as though to someone too simple to survive, that children must be beaten regularly or how else will they learn to do what they're bid? 'And they'd not leave gutties of each other if they weren't bate', he continued. 'They fight the bit in, day in and day out till they have our heads turned, night, noon and morning.'

It never seemed to occur to him that violence breeds violence.

'Do you remember', Sinclare said wonderingly, 'how he *did* beat them? And how often? He beat them with a belt with a buckle on it. And for nothing. I remember once when Rosie was playing up at our house, and her father shouting out for her and she, hearing him, in an immediate panic running down to the Brae towards her house. I followed her, knowing something was wrong, and found him beating her around the legs, great blows with a leather belt with a buckle. She was trying to jump over it as it swung to hit her and she was screaming, but the more she jumped, the more he hit her.'

Once at hay-time he came in from the haggart where stacks were piled just as his eldest son, Francey, dropped from the highest beam of the hayshed; and Francey, seeing him, stayed there petrified and suspended, hanging among the motes and the sun, terrorized out of gravity's pull. When I read, years later, Nijinsky's simple explanation of how he had managed to appear to stop in mid-air during his remarkable leaps, 'I jump and then I stop,' I could still see Francey anchored in mid-air above his father's baleful eyes. His father was unimpressed with the feat. 'Bad cess to you, lepping up there like a buck rabbit,' he shouted. 'You wouldn't do a hand's turn if you were let. Come down out of there or by Jaysus I'll bate the talla out of you.' Francey plummeted, hit the hay and ran dodging out of reach of his father's angry hand.

Now when I hear or read of the astonished queries of adults, when some cruelty to children has come to light, as to why the child did not speak of its suffering nor ask for help, I know they are ignorant of the powerlessness of an abused child. A child accepts, dreadfully accepts, having no means of escape nor means of comparison, whatever hurts are laid on it, though those hurts may last its lifetime and bleed into future, distant lifetimes. And in the behaviour of children to adults and adults to children in our atavistic society I find explanations for many puzzling aspects of social and literary history. We wonder, when reading of how cruelly children were used, how adults could be so heartless and why children were treated so harshly in the past – not only by people who were penniless, pitiful and deprived themselves, but by kind parents who loved their children. We wonder why and how sensibilities have changed so.

All the children in the families around us were brought up according to the system that obtained before the softening and forgiving insights of modern psychology were available or acceptable. The notion of the importance of a child, of his moral and social position in the family, has changed greatly in this century. The concept of the child as a vulnerable, tender and contributing individual was not one that had entered the currency of thinking in our childhood. Even if it had, such a concept has to do with time, money and space as much as with imagination and education; many parents in our district, good devout charitable people though they were, were too ground down by the endless struggle of caring for their ever-increasing families (and forbidden to use birth control on pain of hell-fire) to cultivate the idea of each child as an individual whose demands of the spirit were important and proper, whose creative inclinations were valuable and whose potential was at least as important as what was already there. It was all that many parents could do to feed their children and get them clothed; mothers at night were more often than not collapsing from tiredness with no means of escape; and fathers also collapsed from tiredness, and too often were collapsing from their escape into drink.

All this is not to say that children in our generation were not loved, but they were far more often clouted and beaten than children are nowadays, and they had to fend more for themselves. And the MacAllister children most of all. There were seven children in their family and their father's seasonal occupation as a fisherman, working outside the unfair, monopolistic, fishing laws which obtained at that time on the lough, was his only source of income.

'Did you ever read or see *Padre Padrone*?' Eiram asked me. 'The story of an Italian peasant and his son, in which he beat his child senseless? He loved him. As did Joe-Pat MacAllister love his children. But he was a patriarch and that was how things were run. He was an old-fashioned father, locked in his time.'

Now we would surmise that Joe-Pat himself had been beaten as a child and that he was locked into his own pain. Locked not just in time and pain but also in history, convention, religion, place – left behind while elsewhere the century swept on.

For me that sudden leap of Francey's from the top rafter of the hayshed has pushed everything else that happened in there into a dark shadowy background. He hangs there, poised, taut, for ever about to be punished by the violent adult waiting below who controls his life and who seems to need to vex his children to assuage his own pain. Yet if I look behind that image I see that the background is not dark at all. If I venture back inside I see it is aglow, and that in there is stored a golden granary: those hours of happiness when content in each other's company we found endless diversion, when we jumped dangerously across deep chasms that lay between the teetering stacked bales of straw, when we climbed from beam to beam to look out of the ventilation holes to see the land slipping into the lough, when we played hide-and-seek among the corn stacks, when we lay watching the farm cats suckle kittens in the nests they made in high corners of hay out of reach of dogs and foxes, and when we too made nests in the piled-up hay, thirty feet above ground, sinking into its yielding prickly crispness, so dry it almost burned.

I discover happiness within the curved confines of that high, pink, corrugated-iron building where, through those round holes cut high into each side, just below the sweep of the arched roof, pours a fall of sun so thick and golden, cascading so heavily and continuously through the stoor and dust that where it is trapped by the hay we almost expect an accumulation, a pond of sun, leaking and seeping away into the stiff yellow hay that lay like Rumplestiltskin's gold around us.

4

For each of us the concept of time plays a significant part in our sisterly lives, and the idea of time being relative bore a different gloss under the pressure of our powerful relations. Each one of us passionately insisted on the recognition of an exact span of months separating us, for the indisputability of those extra months in a world where most other things were disputed gave us an advantage over the one who was younger. The span of age between us always retains its monolithic quality; the ordinary flux of time, hastening as it is sucked towards its end, seems to us to part and close around sisterly time as though we are boulders in its stream.

Sometimes as I walked to the lough or lay ensconced in the overgrown tangle of lost land at the top of the haggart in our small farm, hidden from view, though I was privy to the sounds of the men working in the yards and byres I felt I could hear time sliding past in a troubling tempo. It seemed as unnerving as if the waves of the lough had begun to come in sideways to the shore; and this connection with the beat of time brought with it a melancholy sense of the previousness of life, and a horrid sense of haste.

We were all of us often shaken by premonitory turns, which had their genesis in the exemplary foreknowledge of our lives given to us by the sister ahead in time and space. Whatever one did, the sister ahead had already done; wherever one went, a sister had been there; whatever learnt, a sister knew; whatever one experienced, a sister had felt first. We shared so much, yet in our guarded inner lives we were defensively on our own – perhaps dreaming the same dreams or labouring under the same anxieties, but rarely confiding in each other since such confidences always became confessions and were a matter of the finest timing and conjunction of moods. We found it difficult, unless we ourselves were labouring under some parallel grievance, to listen with sympathy to a sister's plaint; her naked need for tender responses often only triggered adverse reactions – irritation, sharpness and shame – since confessional revelations often only sound like complaints or, worse, a parody of all that one is feeling onself,

35

and listening to a sister's grievance reduces the significance of one's own.

Although we always professed that we wanted to be alone, we needed each other as safeguards, bulwarks against the world. We needed each other's physical connivance in the events of our lives if they were to metamorphose into experiences instead of remaining merely happenings with no reality. A sister's presence, response and comprehension were often the only veracity. Yet the gaps between us were too big to cross by efforts at rational thought. They were only bridged by love, by seeking to forgive, by consolation, by each sister revealing painfully that she was as human and vulnerable as the other, and by being accommodated at such moments by the other.

The moment when it first happened to me with Eiram freeze-dried itself with such clarity in my mind that under the lineaments she bears later lives the image of a small, square-shouldered girl with her head on one side, her enormous ribbon flopping, crying outside the post office in Warrenpoint, the small seaside town where our maternal aunt still lives and with whom we go to spend our summer holiday. Eiram is crying, as far as I can make out, because she has to go in to buy stamps for this aunt and she cannot face it, the errand is too unknown, too potentially violating. I go in, because anything is better than to have Eiram crying.

Watching her cry, with a deep uncomprehending sympathy, I feel a small, deep shudder as her authority shifts, as an iceberg might in the merest melting reveal the influence of a warmer current of water suddenly reaching it from far away. Somewhere ahead, I suddenly realize, there are different waters where perhaps we can all melt our differences, and where the years and the spaces between us will not matter. I could never have known how very far ahead those waters lay. But Eiram's crying also frightened me, since she hardly ever cried; her brave defiance makes her almost unable to give in, even when her capitulation begins to seem to be the object of the punishment.

'The devil's in her as big as a goat,' is often said about any recalcitrant child but about Eiram more often than most. As the punishment increased Eiram's lips tightened. Nor would she cry, not even when, worst of all, she was sent out to pick the sally rod to be whipped with. She jumps over the little slashing flail in a serious parody of a skipping-game until eventually the adult, angrier than before, raises the rod high and catches her harder. She is nimble and brave, is Eiram, but she is also timid and only afterwards in the semi-darkness of her room will she let her small, bony face collapse. I want to grasp her to protect her, consume her, to get rid of her, as I want to consume all my sisters, to have them safely, protectedly disappear.

'But such things happen so rarely,' Eiram says gently years later. 'That's why you remember them; because they were utterly memorable and not commonplace at all. So they colour your view.'

Proximity made us privy to each other's secrets or methods of concealment; familiarity made us contemptuously knowledgeable about each other's vulnerabilities and powers, and we could swagger on to each other's territories and know how far to go, and where to go to do it; so each one of us retreated to further secret places. To reveal these secret vulnerabilities by reacting to encroachment and thus admitting that a sister had reached the farthest place in our psyche was something we tried to deny ourselves. And yet the sister was the only person on earth who knew where those places were and how to get there.

These private attitudes were reinforced by those that obtained in our more public world, in which it was also difficult and threatening to reveal ignorance and its mate, fear. Our system of education – moral, cultural and academic, formal and informal – seemed geared to the premise that lack of knowledge was shameful, a thing to be concealed, and as a result of these habits of secrecy and defence we became stubbornly resistant to apprehending our own ignorance or to letting anyone else apprehend it. We concealed gaps in our knowledge as best we could, since admitting ignorance was diminishing and put one at a disadvantage, and might give the other a feeling of superiority and power.

Springing out of these attitudes was a sulky, touchy vanity that had nothing to do with self-esteem. Saying 'I don't know, no I *don't* understand' is easy when you're older or more secure, when you have nothing to lose and knowledge to gain. To be able to say it supposes a measure of trust in the reaction that such an admission is likely to provoke. We were fearful of admitting ignorance, especially at school, being both too insecure in ourselves and too frightened of the teachers, whose tempers were understandably on a short rein trying to teach up to fifty children in one small room. I remember the sensation in that overcrowded classroom one day when the small, ringleted daughter of emigrants, returned from the United States for a triumphant summer holiday and allowed to visit the school as a treat, stared at the first lines of a poem written on the blackboard: 'Abou Ben Adhem, may his tribe increase.' In answer to Miss Rogers's fierce command addressed to the room at large. '*Do* you understand?' (which being interpreted meant, 'You'd *better* understand') she piped that no, she didn't, she had simply no idea. To this glamorous stranger it was a question, nothing more. We were astounded and somehow amused by the complete misinterpretation of the injunction and her misunderstanding of the situation.

We waited for some apocalyptic happening, some retribution to befall the golden child, instead of which Miss Rogers, perhaps equally surprised by the unexpected response, explained what the odd legend meant. But we permanent scholars never tried to emulate that straightforward and unafraid American visitor – talk like that was risky, too near to impertinence, and we lied in our teeth about our comprehension as we chanted lines like 'My love's an arbutus by the borders of Lene' or memorized the rainfall of the Ozarks without knowing what they were, or learned the Lord's Prayer in Irish, which seemed to end with the mysterious words 'a chasing the wolf amen'. We expended considerable effort in contriving not to be noticed at school, since to be noticed was often a matter for rancour or obscure blame. A child who fought back was 'a wee skitter'. I admired with a kind of fearful wonder the bravery of those few of my peers who stood up to the adults that shouted and rebuked them with such colossal, frightening energy.

In this prevailing ethos, the questions asked of children differed only in their emphasis from the genuine questions asked in other systems. But emphasis makes all the difference. 'Who do you think *you* are?' asked to wound, as a reprimand, or as the amazed response to what has been interpreted as conceit, immodesty or the dreaded boldness is very different from the genuine enquiry bent on discovery and exploration: '*Who* do you think you are?'

As small children we were too frightened of the question to analyse it, and we fled from it because it was so often the beginning of humiliation. But as I grew older I raged inwardly against the question and the questioner. Why should our mentors, our teachers, our guides ask the question like this? We knew nothing of our history, of the reductive process of a way of life built on deprivation and poverty, nothing of the cruelty of a religion or a political system that made self-effacement the safest way to live and which took away from a race its ability to esteem itself. Self-effacement as practised among us was as much a political gesture as a religious one – a form not just of modesty but of self-protection. I know, from my own experience, that it covered a raging anger in our race and nation.

The historical necessities of keeping your head down and your eyes averted so as not to attract notice or unwanted attention, a whole system of beaten-in subservience was behind such behaviour as well as that crippling ethic of modesty. This attribute or rather infliction termed modesty is a peculiarly Irish interpretation of the virtue, and it was (and still is) linked and slurred into most nuances of sexual and social behaviour. Modesty as such was supposed to be a fragile thing, easily impaired, but its meaning and interpretation had a horrid tensile strength. In order to remain modest – which was a necessity for women if they were to be respected – sensuality and sensuousness could never be a matter for celebration, but only for denial: all aspects of sex had to be secretive. Exuberance was viewed askance and a belief, however tentative, in one's own importance in the scheme of things must needs be crushed since that was conceit, pretension, delusion or, more often than not, all three at once. In this dispensation most children knew that the quieter they were the more praised they would be – although only in an oblique overheard way – as tractable creatures. The highest praise – 'She's a good wee girl and dis what she's bid,' said sagely by one adult to another – meant only that the child in question made few demands on the speaker. Effacement and quietness became equated with goodness, no new equation in Ireland, where effacement had once contributed to survival.

Requests, mute or spoken, which demanded an emotional response from an adult seemed to upset some hairspring balance of temper, and rather than gaining a sense of their own value many children acquired the painful knowledge that to be a child was to exist in an unlucky state of suspension, something to be stumbled over by adults, blocking their important doings, and in the stumbling both the felled and the one who caused the fall were hurt.

We as a family were more privileged than many of our contemporaries around us: for a start our parents were, relatively speaking, much richer. A teacher's salary, which was guaranteed and steady when most people lived from hand to mouth without any regular income, was riches indeed. And the atmosphere in our home was particularly free from the taint of bigotry and prejudice which so poisoned and continues to poison much of life in Northern Ireland. In fact there was a long tradition of tolerance in both our parents' families, stretching back 150 years – a remarkable tradition, especially within our closed segregated society, where Catholic married Catholic and it was tantamount to sin to marry 'outside' the faith.

Because our grandfather with phenomenal energy and imagination and a feverish ambition for status had battled his way above the crippling lack of expectation in his district, had travelled, made money (much of which he later lost on the stock market) and became the local magistrate, my father's family accepted a wider, more privileged life and education as their due, and so did we. We never doubted that we would go to grammar school, whether or not we passed the eleven plus, a scholarship examination first introduced in the early 1950s and which, if passed, guaranteed financial help and a place at a grammar school. Until its introduction, no matter how intelligent their children, secondary education had simply been beyond the financial reach of most Northern Irish Catholics.

From the first generation given the chance to use their gifts by the institution of this scholarship emerged a group of remarkable men and women: poets, writers, lawyers, civil rights leaders and politicians. But the eleven plus examination was also a brilliantly effective excluder, and it took years before the apparent availability of free further education actually became a reality for the children in Ardboe. Of all those who went to primary school with us, no other girls went on to further education, and our brother was one of only two boys in his generation who passed the examination or, indeed, entered for it.

Leaving them behind, we knew the astonishing talents lying fallow or going to waste among our contemporaries: there were those who were phenomenal musicians, music trickling from their fingers; others who were natural mathematicians and could instantaneously do complicated compound 'sums' in their heads, but who viewed their ability as a trick instead of an innate gift that might be developed or possibly be useful. Many of our peers displayed a fine talent for painting in the occasional scanty hour of 'art' and there was in the school in general an inspired and poetic use of language. None of this talent was nurtured and, when they left school, our contemporaries' futures were even bleaker than the classrooms they had quit. Left to negotiate hopelessly with their imaginations, their intelligences mouldering, left without a future, many people of the district had a double grief: grief for themselves as they were and for the person they might have become. That loss of themselves and their future was monumentally wounding to them, to all our futures, and to Ireland.

'Do you remember that big corrugated-iron hen-house at home, up behind the chestnut trees behind the well?' Eiram asked. 'We lived, after all, in a situation that was very pastoral, green, disordered. And what I unequivocally love about our childhood is its physical and sensual quality. The orchards, the haysheds, the rampars, the green flaxholes, the sound of the balers rising and falling in the air, the sound of iron wheels on gravel behind the horses, the smells from everything. Everything *did* smell more strongly then – the hay, the flax, the cows, the wheat, the apples, the hens – perhaps because we were that much closer to it. . . . I was sitting on the steps leading up to the hen-hut and it must have been a very hot day for I was watching that hotness as though it was palpable, that particular acrid, still, heavy-baked, far, far-away day, and the hens were moving around me. Some were inside the hen-house making those low chawking sounds in their throats, others were out scratching in the dust. It was my Adlestrop.

Yes. I remember Adlestrop–
The name, because one afternoon
Of heat the express train drew up there
Unwontedly. It was late June.

The steam hissed. Someone cleared his throat.
No one left and no one came
On the bare platform. What I saw
Was Adlestrop – only the name

And willows, willow-herb, and grass,
And meadowsweet, and haycocks dry,
No whit less still and lonely fair
Than the high cloudlets in the sky.

And for that minute a blackbird sang
Close by, and round him, mistier,
Farther and farther, all the birds
Of Oxfordshire and Gloucestershire.*

And suddenly it was evening and we were being called to go to bed: and I could hear the MacAllisters down in the hay-yard calling to each other, and the sound of the lough and Tamsie whistling as he was leaving to go home. The sun was still pouring in the window, and the midges were dancing and I was so sad. I was filled with grieving, and somewhere in me I still can grieve for that child. But it's unnecessary, such sadness. That *lacrimae rerum* we suffered from had its spring in the idea of where we were going, and what we were leaving behind, as well as in inherited tendencies. And you can only feel such things when you have the chance to leave them behind. Our yearnings, our searchings were tied to aspiration, and weren't we lucky to be able to aspire? So many of our contemporaries couldn't even do that. There were no possibilities for them – no chance of leaving anything behind. They lived with their sadness, with the knowledge, that what they had was all they were ever going to have,

* Edward Thomas.

and where they were was where they would be to the end of their lives.'

We knew we would have to go to boarding-school. There was a good progressive grammar school and a convent school in Magherafelt some twenty miles away; but there was no transport available, and the grammar school would never for a moment have been considered as a possibility since it was a Protestant school, and for a Catholic child to go to it meant, if not actual excommunication, then certainly a sinful flouting of some absolute truth. Even though we knew boarding-school meant being away from home, its meaning never struck us until the day Elizabeth had to go. We all remember the quality and smell of the day she leaves, remember it with such stricken vividness that for ever after the sounds of harvesting resurrect her departure.

The hay is being cut over in John's Johnny's rampar and the sound of the tractor comes lurching over the low hedges. A thresher and baler are working down in the haggart behind our hayshed, beyond the MacAllisters' house, and the moaning rise and fall of their engines is so linked into the atmosphere that we breathe the sound in, rather than hear it. The front door is open wide so that the yellow and red tiles in the hall are warm from the sun, and the dust-motes dangle and float in the shafts of orange light coming through the bubbly, lozenge-shaped glass at each side of the hall door. Elizabeth is completely dressed in the green of her new school uniform with touches of gold on her school tie, and looks utterly unfamiliar and removed. We envy and pity her. We know something irrecoverable is happening to us all and as she leaves with our father in the car, we cling on to the running-boards until we reach the pillars of the gate to the house. Eiram begins to cry. We watch the car coast down Biddy's Brae, as it once coasted with just four children, and as it passes John-Joe hunkered at the end of his loaning, and at the Cross Roads turns out of sight, we slowly go back home.

'That separation', Eiram said simply, years later, 'broke my heart.'

We tried to join hands, Eiram and I, and to move the ring one circle smaller, but it was no good. Elizabeth's space was always there; and we were always waiting.

5

Our cohesion is not just a matter of a close family feeling or material connections. An outside influence or presence joins us together too, holds us literally in place – Muinterevlin, that ragged, low-lying, silent place in which we were born – and, however we move, the place runs in on us as though to hold us tighter. We still converge on it as often as possible and, as we journey down the Moor Hill Road, we listen intently for the first distant sound of the water. As soon as we can hear it we know we are home, however permanent the place we have come from appears to be. For all of us the lough defines that place on the interior map which makes home uniquely home, so that any other place can always only be somewhere else: a simulacrum of the real place and outside our imaginative grasp.

The name of our townland, one of the thirty that makes up the Parish of Ardboe, is Muinterevlin, meaning in Gaelic 'the country of the Devlins, and the land over which we roam is composed of a body-mould of our forbears, dug and turned into the earth, fertilizing it, flavouring it, and the very soil steeped in us, the surface exuding an aura and an odour of us. The old and heavy earth there seems to be as alive as we are, powered by a different kind of life motion, one that is infinitely slower, each heartbeat lasting decades, but to which we are connected. I sometimes think that if I could put my ear to it at the right time I might catch the throb, just as one glittering day I will see the flower on Lizzie's peony that only blooms every seven years, or find the apocryphal piece of wood petrified into stone by the lough water that I buried each year so long ago.

Muinterevlin reaches further into the lough than any other of the small fingers of land along the shore, all of which tentatively dip in to the water as though not sure of the welcome or depth and then dissolve gently into sedgy watery swamp before giving into the water. The edges are held down by boulders, tussocks, osiers and rushes. Just where Muinterevlin reaches the water it suddenly rears up, into Ardboe Point. It is the only hill on the long side of the lough shore and on its very tip stands the Cross reputed to have been built by St Colman and his monks in the seventh century. Behind it, a small graveyard surrounds the ruins of the monks' small church and almost vanished abbey. The graveyard is our magic playground and the Cross pins it to the ground.

The word Ardboe means 'high cow' in Gaelic, and the most romantic and most often repeated explanation for the name is that the mortar used for building the Cross and church was mixed with the milk of a magic cow, which gave it its staying power. Whatever the source of the liquid used to build the Cross and church, cow milk or lough water, it has been standing there, on the only eminence within ten miles, for over thirteen hundred years. The position of the small primitive group of holy buildings silhouetted against water and sky affects us, and most visitors, to initial stillness and silence. The crumbling arched windows frame the perpetual movement of the small crested waves of the lough, and more often than not the two white swans who nest on the Rock Shore, further round from the Cross Point, swim within the serene arched frame.

The Celtic Cross is an extraordinary monument, towering twenty feet and more above us. It is made of massive stone blocks, and each of the four sides of each great block are carved into panels illustrating episodes from the Bible and the Apocrypha. These carvings were once sharp and detailed but are now blurred into indentations and soft shapelessness by the rain and wind of a millennium. Like many Celtic crosses, the High Cross is ringed by four stone arcs at the junction of the shaft and arms, but two of these arcs have fallen away and lie in fragments at the base of the Cross. For years emigrants leaving for England, Scotland and the Americas have taken a small piece of these sacred stones with them as mementoes of what they have had to leave behind. With the advent of cars and a consequent increase in the number of visitors who also took a piece of the old stone as a souvenir, the Cross began to show signs of damage and the Ancient Buildings Authority have had high railings erected around it to prevent further depradations. At the same time, in the 1930s, an official caretaker was appointed to look after the Cross, the graveyard and the abbey. The job was given to an old great-uncle (everyone in the district is inter-related) who is known for some lost reason as the Needle. He knows the arcane meanings and allegories illustrated in each panel of the Cross, and expounds them in a version handed down orally over the centuries. He is sensible to a fault of his official position and the standing it gives him – or he thinks ought to give him – in the community. He is the official expounder of the meaning of the Cross: its reading.

Returned emigrants, amateur archaeologists, strangers out for a day's jaunt, historians or scholars can easily prevail on him to read it, but it would not occur to him to read it to us, nor to us to ask him. We know he would think it a conceit, a waste of time, so what we learn is what we overhear. Since the Needle speaks our strong local dialect, few listeners from outside the parish can understand more than a few words, but no one's enjoyment seems to be lessened by this lack of comprehension.

The Needle is usually either leaning on his gate watching his small world, meander or cycle by, or is sitting on one of the tombstones surveying the lough and keeping an eye out for the water bailiff. Whenever anyone deemed worthy of having the Cross read arrives at its base, he leaves his vantage point and hurries to the Cross. Getting the keys from about his person is a business: he plunges about the waist and pockets of his ancient trousers and coats, scrabbling among pieces of fishing-line, impaling his fingers on eel-hooks, invoking the Holy Family under his breath and asking St Anthony to help him – this kind of search is called 'hoking'. Finally he finds the keys, opens the padlocked iron gate set into the rails with considerable flourish, steps in, closes the gate and looks out grandly at those left outside the barricade. Favoured visitors are occasionally allowed in with him to look more closely at the carvings. We are permanently banished and lurk outside, derisive but fascinated. There is an anticipatory silence.

The Needle hawks at his throat, spits on the ground, stabs at the Cross with his blackthorn stick, glares at the visitors and begins. He always begins on the East panels. 'The East panels. Here's Solomon, the wise man, axed to judge which of the two women's ba it is; both of them say it's theirs. He has a houldt of the ba by its two legs, here's the two legs.' (He jabs at two faint indentations). 'And here's the sword he's lifting to cleave the child in two. That's to see who's the rightful mother. Whichever mother didn't want the child's head split, she would be the mother.' He looks around as though he has passed the judgement of Solomon himself. Those of his audience who understand some of what he has said murmur in admiration, the others, whispering, ask what he has said. He waits until the murmurs have ceased and stabs this time at the panel above. 'This here's Solomon with all couped round him. Above that Abraham has a lamb by the lugs.'

We love the Solomon story, that ancient marvellous test of mother-love, and savour the dreadful end of Samson and listen half in respect, half in derision, while the Needle, between expositions, beetles at us, trying by facial ferocity to make us go away. He resents our presence deeply, since he isn't explaining the panels for us and has, as he often says only loud enough for us to hear, 'a dale more to do nor talking to childer'; but he knows if he bids us more overtly to depart, his foolish and foreign audience might intervene on our behalf.

One memorable day I found the padlocked gate open and crept in, thrilled and fearful. The great Cross loomed high above me. The road past Treanor's towards our house looked different viewed through bars. I put my hand on the warm stone of the Cross for the first time and suddenly the Needle stepped out from behind it. I leapt with guilt. 'Get out', he said, 'and away up the road with you, you skitter. You're like a musheroon. You couldn't be watched. You're not there one time, but the next time you look you were there all the while.'

We spend a great deal of our time – as much as we can get away from school – by the Old Cross and down by the lough shore. To reach it is a matter of walking four hundred yards along that road edged with a prodigal quantity of wild grasses, fruits and flowers. Hawthorn tumbles over bramble and wild roses, and below these bushes, sedges and wild strawberries grow profusely as well as sorrel, which we eat as part of our daily diet, examining each leaf with deep suspicion for the foamy signs of cuckoo sally. Odium attaches to eating this. We think the foam harbours worms, or rather that it breeds them, that they spring from the foam itself.

This belief in the mysterious, spontaneous generation of worms, eels, serpents is, I discover, a line of thought that reels all the way back through human history and is especially connected to the eels which form the main livelihood for those fishermen who live around the lough. Aristotle wrote, I later read with interest, that eels sprang from mud, and a mediaeval historian called Helmont recommended a curious method of engendering them: 'Cut up two turfs covered with May dew, and lay one upon the other, the grassy sides inwards, and then expose them to the heat of the sun; in a few hours there will spring up an infinite quantity of eels.' One May morning I make this sandwich, but no eels spring up, never mind an infinite quantity, though the lough, alongside which I conduct the experiment, is teeming with them and I can hear them slithering around in the boxes waiting to be sent to Billingsgate fish market in London.

The dusty road, one way and the other, for all its shortness links us to nearly everything that is significant in our geography and landscape, connecting with the Cross and dribbling round the outskirts of the newly-built aerodrome. It widens as it leads towards the more populated and civilized part of Ardboe parish, where it ceases to be our psychic territorial property, our trail, and becomes only another road. That road to the Cross, unravelling so timidly between the fields, often had an undiscovered look with its dusty surface in summer or pot-holed, muddy and rutted in winter. Long after most other roads in the country are black and gleaming in their tarmac coverings, ours is still untouched because Lizzie Treanor, who owns the stretch of road that leads to the Cross, refuses to allow it to be tarmacced. Like Barbara Freitchie, she stands defiant, her nine dogs swirling around her, a cigarette dangling from her mouth, swearing at the steam-roller and its hapless driver, an employee of the County Council who has never been this far into the hinterland before.

We, who are sitting like a row of gremlins on the old Cross mound under its railings, cannot get over this. It is an apocalyptic moment. No one in our experience has ever conceived of defying authority, and for Lizzie to be defying the Government in the shape of a steam-roller seems the most astonishingly foolhardy act. We wait for her come-uppance, for the police to arrive, not

48

leisurely on their bikes as they sometimes do but swooping out of lorries to bear her away. None of this happens: the bemused man driving the steam-roller turns his green and silver monster and goes rolling back up the road, squishing out the surplus tar at each side of the road like an overfilled sandwich, to get some further authority for proceeding. There is no further authority for a while, until finally the County Council slaps a requisition order on the road and has it tarred into conformity, while Lizzie stares, baleful, baffled, from her windows.

Along the length of the road, tarred and untarred, sleeping dogs lie like punctuation. Each house has at least one dog attached to it. They are not house pets, but are tolerated and fed scraps. These dogs all have a lean and feral look, and even when they appear to be in a deep sleep in the middle of the road they sense our approach and twitch a tail in greeting and goodwill. The dog belonging to the Dallys is the exception, Argus-like in its wakefulness. It sidles along behind the hedge, keeping abreast but hidden from us, and then at a suitable moment and gap lunges out at our ankles. The Dally dogs come and go, but each looks exactly like the other and seems to have acquired the meanest characteristics of the previous one, as though somehow it absorbed loose dog-spores left behind.

Pad Dally's putative nephew Nealy is often sitting on a boulder at the foot of his loaning watching the stalking attack with a sardonic grin, not unlike the one on the face of his dog. The more mutilated ankles about, the better he likes it. It is one of his few pleasures in life. Every day after school he has to spend heavy hours fetching drinking water from our well, carrying it in buckets suspended in a yoke over his shoulders. We are sorry for him. While the rest of us are in a group headed to the Cross and the lough shore, he has to stay within reach of his aunt's call. It appears that she cannot tolerate the idea of his having a life in any way independent of her and her misery. Our group varies in size from just two of us sisters, to twenty or more children in pairs and trios according to age, and to every group each tract of the road has a specific use and meaning and mystery.

Although there are so few cars in the district – only our parents, the parish priest and his curate own one – there are petrol stains in the potholes along the road making marvellous, shimmering colours. Eiram attempts both to test the bravado of Franky O'Neill – the biggest boy and the villain of our group – and to do away with him, by daring him to drink the glimmering petrol-stained water. 'We believed it was deadly, and so did he, but he knelt down and lapped it up all the same and survived. You'll not remember. Still it shook us and our beliefs badly.' That 'You'll not remember' is the remark of an older sister, but I do remember him well, although he and his parents emigrated to England while I was still very young. I have his description on the tip of my tongue: his shock of black hair, his famous badness, and most of all his rancorous tongue. I was wearing a red velvet bonnet – a pixie hood it was called – trimmed with white fur sent by an aunt who was a nun and headmistress of a school in California, when I most remember him. 'Santy's come early the year,' he said, moving his head in a mirth I could see was almost painful in its intensity, when I bashfully appeared in it, knowing full well that I looked an amadan. The jibe lacerated me, and I never would wear the hood again.

'I look like Santa Claus,' I wept to Ellen, who was trying to make me wear it. *Housewives' Choice* was on the wireless, which meant I was going to be late for school, but I wouldn't let her put it on me. Ellen was puzzled. Usually it was Eiram, Morgan or Nell who became obsessive, suddenly stubborn, about some garment they would no longer wear, no doubt also because of the jibes of some peer. 'He said I looked like Santa Claus,' I muttered at last, reluctant to reveal the depths of my vulnerability and humiliation. 'Who's he?' she said. 'The cat's father?'

'Franky O'Neill.'

'Him?' she said. 'Sure he knows nothing. All he is, is an amadan and a playboy, now give me head peace, and put your new pixie hood that your aunt, so good, sent you, on to your head.' She tied it too tightly under my chin and I took the bundle of sticks I had gathered the night before for the teacher to light the classroom fire with, the tears of humiliation spilling out of that reservoir that I keep topped up and lipping full behind my face, the better to give veracity and authenticity to the sob stories that are so precious a part of the freight in my mind. I ran out past the carved pillars, through the wrought-iron gates, down Biddy's Brae to try to catch the others before they turned the corner at the Cross Roads and left me irrevocably behind. I hated passing Biddy's house on my own. It was isolated from the other houses and its proximity to the road scared me – there were only six or seven houses along that stretch of road leading in the opposite direction from the Cross towards the Cross Roads; most of them are set back from the road up in the rampars and fields, at the end of grassy lanes which we call loanings. Like many in the parish, all these houses are built in the local traditional style: long, low, and white-washed with lime inside and out. They have only one outside door, which is made in two halves, the bottom half always closed against dogs and draughts and over which, if you're tall enough, you can lean for a bit of a crack or to pass the time of day with anyone passing who is temperamentally and psychologically capable of speech. Just inside this door there is a jamb wall to stop the draught from blowing into the kitchen as well as to make a tiny hallway, and all walls, inside and out, are over a foot thick and sliced by small deep windows. There are no more than three rooms in all such houses, including the kitchen, and no inside bathrooms or lavatories; yet many contain families of ten or twelve people of all ages and generations.

In the MacAllister house live seven children, their parents and their grandmother; the Corrans have ten children; and in Pad Dally's house next to them live four old brothers – Joseph, Eddie, Tom and Pad – as well as Teasie, Pad's wife, and his six children and the dog-owning nephew Nealy. Only Pad is married; the other three brothers, like so many of that generation, have continued to live where they were born. As they grow older, they grow more and more wraithlike and silent.

The Corran family, who live next to them and under the same roof, make up for their neighbours' silence by their noisy volubility. There are ten Corran children: the older boys fish on the lough, the older girls work in the Daintyfit bra factory in Cookstown, and the younger brothers and sisters walk to school with us. Even though they are radically different in habits and temperament, the Dallys and the Corrans co-exist peacefully because of the mutual scrupulous regard for territorial rights. The walls of these long, low, shared houses are thick enough – made as they are of mud and stone – to prevent any noise seeping through and, although there are no hedges or fences between the two houses, each family has a strict regard for physical boundaries. Most of the houses in the district look utterly at one with the surrounding landscape and the earth in which they are almost rooted, since they have been built out of the clay beneath them. They look like moulds for houses, rather than the houses themselves.

There are a few notable exceptions to this intimate organic style of local houses. First the pair of tiny cottages built by the Tyrone County Council in 1926: one for the Needle, as part of his job as caretaker of the Cross, in which he lives with his wife and at one time with their ten children, who are all now grown-up and have emigrated, and the other for his brother and equally large family, only two of whom are left at home. These cottages have a mean and alien look with their flung grey pebble-dash clinging so scantily to the rigid four-square walls, although inside they are much lighter than the traditional houses, because of their bigger aluminium windows which open outwards.

Then there's our house, which is the biggest in the townland, a two-storey Edwardian affair with bathrooms, a breakfast-room, a sitting and dining-room. Most exceptional of all, it is surrounded by a large garden, lawns and orchards. My grandfather, who built the house, used the biggest and best of the fields of his small farm to make his house and garden, and in a place where families are so large and land is so scarce such prodigality is extraordinary. In later years we speculate that this house and garden with its orchards, chestnut trees and conifers – alien trees in the landscape – its big lawn, its drive cutting through lugubrious laurels to wrought-iron gates hanging on squat stone pillars topped by spheres, must have seemed like the height of pretension to my grandfather's peers and kin, who would on the whole have wished him ill rather than well, albeit in a mild way. It is often the way of those who have been exploited to begrudge their own kind success.

The third exception is Biddy's house, the one I fear passing and which fronts almost directly on to the road. It is built of stone and has a corrugated tin roof, and her street – the small area

52

covered in stones and pebbles that lies directly in front of every house – is dirty and littered with rubbish and hen-droppings, and slops and old buckets. Her cottage is too near the road for our peace of mind and we always pass by on the other side. But it is also unique because of its decrepitude and squalor. All the other houses in the district (again except ours) are shining, sparkling clean, and full of order, care and a sense of ceremony. Their red-tiled floors are scrubbed daily, the scalloped brass edging on the lintels and mantels polished, the pottery Alsatian dogs or ladies in crinolines, won at the annual fun-fair, dusted and rubbed, and the two universal icons of the intertwined faiths of the district – the oleograph of the Crucifixion and the Irish Declaration of Independence, hanging above the settle – are regularly adjusted. Behind these are wedged the rush crosses made every St Brigid's Day.

Biddy's house looks as though it has not been cleaned in generations. It is a place of darkness, smoke, mutterings and imprecations. Biddy herself is more often than not lurking at the half-open door, her eyes rolling terribly in her grimy face, her hair starting from her head in matted, whitish locks. As we go past she slams the door. 'She can reeve a door the best I ever knowed,' Francey MacAllister says, quite unfazed.

The MacAllisters are more courageous than we are (except perhaps for Eiram and Morgan, who have a wild courage mixed with great timidity), and Biddy to them is an old mad woman, whereas we are put about to live so near someone who tallies with our idea – engendered by illustrations in books – of a witch. She makes manifest our threatening world of fantasy, and this is profoundly scaring; for it she exists, what does not? The idea of Biddy becomes another supernatural terror to add to the ever-increasing hoard and horde of terrors and devils in our minds. On an ordinary, natural level, too, we are frightened of her because she seems to simmer with hate. 'She would put the evil eye on you as soon as look at you,' Ellen warns us, and we scuttle past, avoiding looking at her lest one dreadful cyclopic eye cleave to us like a shiny, dreadful wart.

She is a widow, and her children became deranged or came to some sort of sorry end. Her only surviving daughter, Lena, regularly tries to drown herself in a shallow spring well which lies down the Brae Hill, along the loaning that leads to our low-lying meadows. The MacAllisters tell us about it with considerable relish. Nothing is forbidden to their ears and we rely on them for all illicit information. 'She goes off the head in the morning, any morning, no rhyme nor reason nor warning', Francey MacAllister says, 'and away down the road and throws herself into the well. She's not too daft though, for she does it at a time when she thinks somebody will soon be passing.' Once or twice, however, no one is passing and she has to haul herself out, wringing wet, and go back up the hill to her sad existence and her tormented, demented mother. Joe-Pat MacAllister, Francey's father, has met her twice in this condition, dripping with tears and spring water, and has reluctantly led her home – which is how Francey knows. We never doubted the story.

I think of her often and try to transpose the image of Millais' beautiful Ophelia (a reproduction of which hangs in our dining-room) over the lineaments of the deranged woman I know. I try, too, to invest her pathetic suicide attempts – so patently, so manifestly a call for help, even to us who have never heard of psychology – with some kind of usefulness, some beauty or truth or romance. Poor, fat Ophelia. Over the floating Millais image drifts a truer one – the image of Lena trying to insert her big, awkward body into the shallow well, her lank, short hair, her mottled legs. These images mingle with the image I see when the haylifter drawn by Nellie, our huge Clydesdale mare, and captained by Tamsie who works on our farm, with all of us – Corrans, MacAllisters, Dallys and Gallaghers, over twenty children – lying on it rumbles across the wide ditches called keshes that moat and drain the meadows, bridged by heavy sleeper logs laid side by side with tufty grasses and weeds growing out of the spaces and cavities between them. These makeshift bridges have no railings or raised edges and are at a right-angle to the approach loaning. They are only a scant foot wider than the iron-wheeled haylifter so that there is little room for the fine negotiation of horse and machinery across the bridge.

Our view of what is happening ahead is blocked by Nellie's enormous cleft rump, but lying with our heads over the edge and watching how Tamsie gauges the horse's movements to a nicety we feel that with one slip of judgement the haylifter, the horse and all of us will be arse-over-tip into the green water below. We half hope that this will happen and half dread it, and those who don't have the bottle to stay on during the manoeuvres often jump off before we reach the kesh, pretending, as they jump, to be casual. Sometimes Tamsie shouts at us to get off anyway, but since we are half-deafened by the rattle of the iron wheels on the rough road, a noise that shakes our teeth in our heads, we don't hear him. We exaggerate this rattling and shaking sensation by humming with our lips pursed, so that the combined noise sounds in our own ears like insects, prehistoric in size. Tamsie leans backwards, feet braced, his muscles bulging as he guides and plays the reins, whistling a narrow tune between his teeth, and the tune gets narrower as the haylifter budges and turns and scrapes and the iron wheels sink into the moss. The whistle becomes a hiss or a low clucking sound as Nellie backs up and inches forwards, and backs up again, and then as her iron-plated hooves sound out on the hollow boards the whistle expands into full tune and we know that ww are safe.

The most thrilling part of the whole idea of the collapse of the haylifter into the thin lagoon below is the idea of the living mound that is Nellie falling into the water. She is colossal and so is her harness. The fat leather collar, so heavy that none of us can singly lift it and on to which are shackled the brass blinkers and harness, the bit and braces, and the straps and bands that support the haylifter – all would have made the displacement of water terrific. There are those cynics among us who say that Nellie has manoeuvred herself and her burden so often over the kesh that she could do it by herself, which canard throws Tamsie into a rage. For me, the whole thing hinges on Tamsie and his lore.

Tamsie's surname is Devlin and he is kin, indeed as is nearly everyone in the district – we are all at some remove interrelated – and he has worked on the farm for soolong that he is an integral part of our background. Ellen has been having a walk-out with his brother Joe for years, but this is never referred to by either Tamsie or her, although he eats the meals she has cooked for him in our kitchen for years.

He died last year, this keeper of the horses (the meaning of Devlin in Gaelic), a tiny, washed, skeletal figure with enormous, globular eyes set in a pearly, hollow face. I never saw such mortality. He is in charge of the horses, the two Clydesdale mares Nellie and Bess, and their mate, a stallion aptly enough called Dick, who occasionally breaks out of his stable and goes snorting across the yard in search of some sexual dream of his own. Once, when he was coupled into the haylifter, he suddenly reared into the air, an enormous column of flesh and flash, and took off; imprinted in my head is the moment when Dick and the haylifter went careering across the field towards a hedge with Tamsie straining on the reins shouting and cursing and imploring the Holy Ghost to intervene to prevent all being couped and him being kilt.

Not long afterwards, walking past the fairy tree on our straggly way home from school a mile away and right outside our territory, we suddenly hear a horse come running up the hill, its hooves making wild and dreadful music on the tarmac. We jump the nearest ditch, run across the fields mute and sweating and, as we reach the dense boundary ditch on the other side of the field and begin to fight through, we stop, suspended in our panic just for an instant, and look back, dreading that the horse has jumped the hedge and is following us, its hooves muffled by the grass. To our terror it has indeed stopped its headlong flight up the hill and, tossing its head and mane, appears to be glinting over to where we are battering our way through the quick-thorn hedge. All this is exaggerated, I must suppose, superimposed images crowding on to what actually happened, but I do remember with clarity the utter relief of Eiram being with me. No matter how much I pretend to be independent of her, and although in many ways she appeared to be dependent on my courage in unknown situations, she is always out there ahead of me, testing the ground, and I am attached to her by an invisible safety-rope.

There are curious aspects to our several, singular stories and memories of horses in our childhood, for each of us remembers one incident with awful clarity, yet no one else shares that particular memory. Eiram remembers it was partly because she was alone that her encounter with horses was particularly terrifying. 'I was rarely lonely, and indeed being alone seemed such a luxury that I feel I couldn't have been alone. And yet I know I was. It was a sunny afternoon and I was coming home from school – the rest of you must have walked on – and suddenly I heard the sound of a horse and trap coming over the hill like the Ride of the Valkyries, a dreadful, out-of-control clattering bearing down on me. I pressed against Rosy Campbell's wall in terror and suddenly there it was – a horse and a trap and its driver, the man who sold paraffin and thick oil from a tank in the back. He was standing up in the trap with a funnel on his head and the oil dripping down his face over his clothes. I was so terrified that I couldn't move and I feared he would stop. I see it for ever. A horse galloping; a madman holding the reins; a funnel on top of his head; the oil down his face – oh, the poets haven't written about the horse as an archetype for nothing. Poor man; he was committed to Omagh shortly afterwards, and escaped and jumped in front of a tram and was killed.'

Such events change the reality and idea of horses for us from being stolid amiable creatures like Nellie who, while her haylifter is being unloaded, accepts the clumps of grass we tear up and push behind the big bit in her mouth, into magic animals shying in strange grass, unpredictable and potent.

Once inside the meadow we chase white butterflies, catching them and putting them into a jar. Each of these butterflies, it is rumoured by the naturalists among us, lays forty eggs which will turn into caterpillars and devour cabbages.

'That's forty more cabbages saved,' Elizabeth says savagely as she slaps another delicate pinioned creature into her overcrowded jam-jar. She hates cabbage, indeed we all do and we don't care if every cabbage in the country is laid low by these white ethereal butterflies, but we are filled with a lust to hunt, to have an objective, to capture.

While we are racketing around with our jars, the men are levering the haystack up off its foundations of crossed sally branches and on to the steel edge of the haylifter which is now tipped back on to the grass. Tamsie gives the peculiar low noise in his throat that makes Nellie start a ponderous reverse and the end of the haylifter knifes under the stack; the men leap upwards and pull down on the shafts with all their weight, bringing the whole thing back to harness-level; the stack tilts and thuds on, Nellie shudders with its sudden settled weight and the journey back to the hayshed begins again. We are not encouraged to ride back on the full haylifter unless we can find somewhere to cling on to at the front, between the shafts and out of reach of Joe-Pat's somewhat malicious feet. Sometimes I stay on in the meadow by myself, and watch as the haylifter with its burden rumbles over the kesh. The haystack drips over the edges like golden summer icicles and, as the laden wagon turns after having crossed the kesh, Nellie's great body comes into profile, her rump gleaming. Even from this distance it is the most solidly circular object I have ever seen, the living definition of a sphere, the skin stretched in a great taut arc over the compacted muscle and bone, and the flesh curving melodiously underneath, moving with a steady intimate rhythm, in a ripple of time.

As they disappear out on to the road and Tamsie's whistle grows fainter, the meadow takes on an astonishing air of desertion. It is a world on its own and in that vast, quiet space surrounded by the narrow channels of water I crave something with such desperation that it marks my mind with its memory, just as the vaccination I was given as a baby still marks my thigh to show my immunization from some virulent threat. My craving is the common one, but to me it is unique: I want redemption, or restoration, some external stilling of my unquiet soul. I do not, cannot, know what it is I am yearning for; I can only formulate it in the terms and words of morals and religion. I want to be at an end, and I want to be good. At the crisis of such moments I vow with an exultant desperation that I will become a nun, since that is my only known conjunction of both desires, the only equipment I have for reconciliation. Surely, I think, these yearnings and clamourings are what our priests and teachers have warned us we must listen out for as the first priority in our lives, the small insistent voice of God calling us to serve him, but calling in a whisper – our vocation. A kind of wild grief comes over me when I contemplate the idea of my withdrawal from the world. Yet I know that the world is a wicked place and my passion for it is evidence of Satan's power of seduction, and the more I love it the more am I in danger of losing my own soul. We live on a

58

horrid knife-edge of loss, and are almost always, it seems to me, in danger of losing our souls. It's a hateful threat hanging over us, and it contains such endless imaginings, such Macbeth-will-sleep-no-more ramifications that there is no escaping it. I think it is no coincidence that so many Catholic children brought up in their fierce, slipping, uneasy dispensation are so obsessive about losing and finding things, and so jealous of what is their own.

As I stand in the meadow trying to listen and trying not to hear, I find it puzzling and deeply unfair that whereas so many of God's messages and strictures are delivered to us in ringing tones and injunctions as absolute truths with no possibility of being unheard or misinterpreted, this important individual message about one's vocation, which could mean the difference between spiritual life and eternal death, should be delivered in such a forlorn little whisper, easily unheard in the clatter of daily life.

I do not stay behind in the meadow too often, for although I am drawn to its wide deserted emptiness, the flatness of the stubble stretching towards the dark thorn-hedges, the pale glimmer of the boundary canals, the silence broken only by peewit and corncrake calls, I do not know what to do with the contingent onrush of pain. It is perhaps to feel the melancholy descending that makes me stay behind, as much as my love for the look and feel of the place. As a child will probe a sore tooth as a reminder of what it has suffered or could suffer, I tiptoe towards my incipient feelings of desolation, create the conditions in which I will again feel as desolate as when I first felt abandonment. Once I touch the tender spot, pain comes flooding in and I don't know what to do with it: it flows along my veins and lies in my stomach like dirty rainwater in a gutter. Then, I can hardly wait for the haylifter to come back again, and on the next return journey I am up there with my sisters pretending not to hear Joe-Pat swearing at us to get off, clinging to the front as the lifter rattles and sways over the meadow and across the kesh and up past John-Joe crouched as always on his hunkers at the bottom of his loaning.

'You'd wonder he didn't get a hardening of the joints, some kind of stiffening,' Tamsie said whenever he saw him. We waited for the apocalyptic day when he would try to unfold his length and discover that he couldn't, that he had folded himself once too often and found his body permanently hardened into creases. It never happened. He would rise easily, long and limber, and set off up his loaning, and into the little tin-roofed house by the lough shore, which none of us had ever been allowed inside. We could only speculate as to whether he sat on a chair or lay down on a bed or continued, even in his own seclusion, to squat on those iron thighs.

John-Joe's loaning was a living paradise for a child, a deep green alleyway made narrow by the lushness of vegetation, overgrown by trees and hedges and lined with high banks of wild herbs and wild flowers. Under this sweet cover grew wild strawberries which some of us threaded on to a long stalk of sedge grass the better to savour them all at once. The more prodigal ate them one by one. I always threaded mine, grading them carefully, making a marvellous mouth-watering necklace – and then generally dropped it, lost it, fell into a cowpat with it, or engaged in some other early form of self-inflicted deprivation.

When I was an infant, perhaps five years old, I set off on the small tricycle which was the communal toy and, having puffed my way up the loaning, climbed off and set about searching for the strawberries. When I had picked a stalkful I went back to the tricycle well enough pleased with myself and found Lena standing beside it. I sensed her strangeness and tried to back away, but she reached for me and took the strawberries from my hand and, tilting her throat, put the full stalk deep into her mouth. Silent and frightened I climbed on to the tricycle and tried to pedal away, but she was beside me on all fours, feral as Dally's dog, her mouth red with the juices of the strawberries, and she sank her teeth into my hand so that they met through my flesh.

As we pass the well and her mother's house, I question Tamsie as to what finally happened to Lena. It transpires that one day two policemen on one of their rare bicycle excursions into our district found her in the well, lifted her out and had her committed to the lunatic asylum in Omagh.

'Going to Omagh' means only one thing in our vernacular – that you are irrevocably off your head. Adults, especially teachers and mothers, scream at us when we have got on their nerves that we'll have them in Omagh afore we're through, and it is a severe warning. But the manifestations of madness have to be very intrusive and obvious indeed before Omagh looms, since a high proportion of those who live around us are, as a result of isolation and inbreeding, extremely odd in their behaviour and manner and even in their looks. No one passes any remarks on these people who are nudged by faith, fate and chance and wounded by circumstances and inbreeding into a secondary, lost, odd world of fantasy within the lost, odd, world that is primary reality, that is our place of birth and theirs of death.

6

Although she bore seven children within ten years, my mother only stopped teaching for a short time before and after each of our births. Soon after Elizabeth was born, Ellen came to work for her in the house and remained with us until we had all left home.

Ellen always seemed to me to be ageless, fixed in a time of her own, infinitely powerful and adult; but I realized as I grew older that she must have been a very young girl, only fifteen or sixteen, when she first came to live with us. She was fixed in our early lives at the centre of the domestic life of the house, and she cooked and cleaned and looked after us with the household – and there were usually three children under five years of age at any one time.

We love Ellen and she is good to us, but she has suffered too much in her own vexed, hardly gone childhood and now has too much to do to be able to dole out the kind of time-consuming attention and understanding that we crave. Instead of reassurance we are sometimes given the opposite by the women in our lives, for antique reasons stretching back through generations of vexed adults who, having not themselves received consolation, inflict much the same hurt on children as was visited on them in the appalling dependency of childhood. Our childhood is riddled with stories told by adults who sometimes laugh as they tell them, although in that laughter we recognize pain – the pain of desperation that underlies most Irish humour. The black mixture makes for an irony that is cruel and crippling in its hardness, yet susceptible to corrupting sentimentality.

Ellen's stories become part of our family lore and, as in the larger folklore of Ireland, the oral tradition and the way in which she tells them keep alive the immediacy and pain of the moment, and perhaps exaggerate it. Vicarious suffering is very keen, and some of the stories Ellen tells us without comment illustrate the cruel and jealous peevishness that many adults of the time and place showed towards children. She never tells the stories as laments or with regret or grief, but rather as anecdotes, far-off things that happened to her or her family; she accepts them as part of life, but hearing them left us with a great fear of the cruelty of circumstance and passion, and the arbitrary ways of adults. She told us of the kittens she had loved and hidden that had been drowned in front of her eyes; of things destroyed that she cherished; of pigs slaughtered in the backyard of the house, the children watching the slaughter with acceptance, although the killing was slow and bloody because the pigs made bids to escape even when their stomachs were already slit. One story in particular grieved us and made us want to protect her: 'The one and only doll she ever had in her life . . .,' Eiram said. 'She told me about it years and years after it had happened, and when she was telling me she began to cry.' As Eiram spoke, she too began to cry.

'She got a doll in a parcel from America from an aunt who had emigrated. She couldn't believe it, the fact of the doll and the fact that it was only hers. She ran out of the house in excitement to show it to whoever she could find, to share the astonishment. There was an old man clipping the hedge just down the road, and he heard her laughing and shouting, and called her and said, "Show us the doll." She handed it up to him and he clipped the head off the doll with the shears and threw it back to her. She never had another doll in her life.'

In all the years Ellen works for us I hardly ever see her sit down except quickly after our tea-time, before she makes our parents' evening meal. She is constantly on the go, and more often than not snatches her meals as she moves about, or leans against the dresser with a mug of tea in her hand abstractedly staring ahead, as though uninterested in what is being said around her but avid all the same for any fragment of news. She seems always to be surrounded by pulsing vibrations, as though something fraught and doom-laden, although ultimately pleasurable, is impending, lying in wait among the flour sacks or under the surface of the cream in the crocks in the scullery – brown crocks with a deep yellow glaze dribbling down their sides, made in Coalisland near where she was born twenty miles away.

She works like a fury from early morning till late evening and cooks for all of us: children, Tamsie, the extra farm-workers and my parents. Often when she has finished cooking my parents' meal she tells us with heavy irony to carry the food in to the gentry. They eat in the dining-room; we eat in the kitchen at wooden tables which she scrubs to a bleached whiteness every day or, if there are too many men in the kitchen at harvest time, we eat in the breakfast-room.

Ellen spends a great deal of time redding-up, which is trying to get her kitchen in order; perhaps once a month things actually do get redd-up to her satisfaction, but most of the time she is working towards that point. All through meals we hold on to our plate lest it be whipped away and the table redd-up before we have finished. It seems to us that Ellen rather likes her preparations, and her food, to be beset by some small disaster. Indeed, ever since she first heard my mother use the word 'desserts' to describe the semolina, rice and tapioca puddings that Ellen reluctantly makes in order to use up the milk sent from the milking-byres morning and evening, she has called them 'disasters', which she imagines is both ironic word-play and a dig at my mother's pretension. But when a small, sophisticated cousin who came to stay agreed gloomily, 'They *are* disasters, aren't they,' Ellen was stung to the quick.

Once that same sophisticated cousin (the daughter of my father's brother, who had become a doctor) took one of Morgan's toys away from her. Morgan howled impotently and Ellen waited for the cousin's mother to bid the child return it immediately, if not sooner, which was how Ellen liked such things to be done. The mother, however, quite oblivious to the whole affair, did not do so and Ellen, affronted, waited until the cousin crawled near her and punished her by seizing the toy, pinching the child, and warning her – putting her face very close to the child's and narrowing her eyes – not to bother telling her mother of the retribution.

'Nasty thing,' the traitorous child said loudly and scuttled off to tell her mother. The expression became Ellen's byword – uttered in a mincing voice – for insult and cheek and boldness or for someone who had stepped out of some mysterious line of her own.

'Did you *see* her?' she would ask, scandalized and jealous, if anyone came to Sunday Mass in any version, however muted, of any new fashion. 'All dolled up, making a show of herself the nasty thing, how would she have the face to wear it?' But there was always a note of yearning in her voice at such times.

All the same, the cousin has a point about the disaster, since not only are the puddings themselves curious affairs but their very making is fraught with drama and excitations. Ellen pours the milk into the saucepan on the range and stands over it, dipping a suspicious finger into it and watching it as a cat watches a fly buzzing in a window. More often than not there are blisters on all her fingers since this is her only way of testing her cooking temperatures. As soon as the milk begins to get hot she gives up her vigilance or loses patience and goes rushing off into the scullery muttering, 'A watched pot never boils.' At this point the milk, as though released from the pressure of her stare, cascades over the edge in a white foam, breaking on the hot surface into skittering white bubbles and releasing that acrid, pervasive smell. The noise frightens the cat out from among the kindling under the range and Ellen, galloping back in from the scullery, swearing blind, usually falls over it as it tries to escape out of the back door. 'Bad cess to you and your breed, seed and generation', she says as she rights herself and grasps the saucepan.

Tamsie, with whom Ellen wages a subtle warfare, is always delighted to happen on these set pieces of kitchen-theatre, and whistles slyly as she mops up and makes a studied point of not looking at the battle area. 'You're redding up the milk then?' he enquires gently, rubbing his nose on his cupped palm. 'Quare smell, burnt milk.'

There is one memorable occasion when he comes sidling in for his midday meal and finds that Ellen has forgotten to put the potatoes on 'for the dinner'. Potatoes are not regarded as a vegetable but as a basic food, almost sacred in their importance, and around their white floury centre are piled the other votive offerings of the meal – boiled cabbage, ham, fried eels, a grunt or tench, or in later years perhaps a sausage or chop when the butcher has called in his van. One of the remarkable things about the meals Tamsie and Ellen share is the amount of daily discussion concerning the quality, size and taste of the potatoes, which they talk about with the same reverence as connoisseurs discuss wine. (The bonus, for us, of potatoes being so important to our nutrition is that our school closes for two weeks in October so that we can help with the potato-picking, which we don't do.) So Ellen's having forgotten the potatoes is a godsend to Tamsie, a unique lapse which he never allows her to forget.

The variations on the same theme are subtle and vary from day to day; neither Ellen nor Tamsie ever acknowledges openly that an elaborate form of teasing is taking place. One day the tease might take the form of Tamsie pronging a potato and beginning to peel it silently while Ellen watches suspiciously, pretending to be busy folding tea-towels.

'You've done the spuds the day then,' he'd finally say. 'You got them on at the latter end.'

'I did', she'd say, 'and divil may they choke you,' and she'd rush into the scullery rolling her eyes. Another day he would begin to peel them smiling, and addressing the potato tenderly: 'She minded to put you on.'

Sometimes the warfare would become more open. It would begin with a kind of idle sarcasm that would not seem offensive to an outsider unversed in the subtle gradations of moods and tones (the packaging of the words as it were), which conveyed the message as much as the message itself.

'What's this scowder?' he says, peering at anything that is not utterly familiar. 'It's a class of a dinner.' Ellen looks away into the mid-distance, as though both question and questioner are below her notice. Tamsie raises a fork of food to his mouth and holds it there poised, and the ensuing dialogue would appear to any casual listener to have suddenly veered radically away from the point under discussion.

'Do you mind Cassie's Dymphna, God love her, and the scone of bread?' he'd ask of the ceiling, or any one of us who happened inadvertently to pass through the kitchen. We have to be surreptitious about our presence in the house during the course of one of these running battles, otherwise we may be enlisted by one side or the other and used as hostages.

'I do mind it well,' Ellen said. 'Haven't you told it a hundred times till my head's turned listening to it. And it wasn't that good a story the first time.'

'She made the bread,' he continued smoothly. 'It was well known she couldn't make bread, so she shouldn't have been at it in the first place. But she would do it, and she put it in the oven and she took it out two hours later and it's safe to say that you couldn't have split it with a sledge-hammer. It was hard, and it was heavy, and it was flat, and she showed it to Feily and she said, oh modest enough, it must be over thirty years ago now, but I mind it well and she said, "Did I miss it Feily?" Anxious. She wanted him to tell her it was all right. "Aye", he said, "you missed it and you missed it badly," and he threw it at her. It would have killed her if it had hit her.' He nodded sagely. 'There's some as good at making dinners around her as Dymphna was at making bread.'

The point of the story was hardly lost on Ellen who enjoyed humour and wit, even at her own expense. Indeed she simultaneously relished and was maddened by anything that deviated from her idea of the norm in behaviour, clothes, vocabulary, accent, although her norm was unusual by most standards.

She is full of saws. If a piece of food falls on the floor she remarks as she lifts it, 'Clean meat never fattened a pig'; or, wiping something with her flower-sprigged overall, 'What the eye doesn't see, the heart doesn't grieve after'; or if we ask for a larger helping of food than we eat, she says with satisfied rancour, 'Your eyes are biggern your gut.' Anyone who asks for more is called a 'gorb'. If we complain about a smell in the kitchen she is triumphant. 'A black dog smells its own dirt first' – which preempts further discussion; and any even faintly ambitious talk or desire is 'hairy talk for baldy people'.

Any child who offends her strict territorial sense or her acute but arbitrary sense of propriety is called a 'skitter', but the written word can never convey the dramatic glottal stop in the middle which gave the epithet such sibilant power. Whenever any of us so far forget ourselves as to use the word 'thought' in a proffered excuse, her face became quite suffused with pleasure. 'You thought did you?' she'd say, her voice full of derisive contentment. 'Do you know what thought did?' We would allow that we didn't know, since each time thought behaved differently. 'Thought stuck a feather in the ground and thought it would grow a hen'; 'thought thought it could fly on one wing.' There was no end to thought's foolishness.

The use of words that did not form part of her own vocabulary gave her equal fuel for spleen and ridicule, foreign words to use as weapons against what she considered pretensions. Many of the words she used have long been lost to everyday English or their pronunciation has altered; in her vocabulary and in ours, the underarm is an oxter, fallen is couped, and opposite is fornenst; the words for quantities are different too – a few objects are called a lock, a few more are a wheen, and we all know the fine difference between such quantities. Wind is pronounced wynd, tea is tay, a broody hen is a clocking hen. She never tells us to stop doing anything; she demands that we quet it, and if any one doesn't hear her injunction, or pretends not to, she enquires if they are deef.

A proughal or a tackle is a derisive term for a person who has failed to do something he or she has boasted to do, or who has given up on the larger issues of life. All drunkards are proughals; and any man who is not married and who lets his eyes rest on her in any significant fashion is a playboy; things that are broken are cleft or riven; and if we come in complaining of being cold or hungry she agrees we are foundered or famished or perished, depending on the severity of the weather or the hunger. (She doesn't agree and tells us to give over.) She is particularly susceptible to shades of facial expression, and when we are smiling in a particularly irritating way – generally at another sister's small misfortune – she pounces on us for girning; yawning is ganting. Any form of hesitation is called kiffling and if one of us asks her to do something which she considers to be outside her bailiwick or below her notice she says 'I will well,' which means exactly the opposite. 'I don't give a hait' is her way of expressing ostensible indifference but is always followed by a threat; if any one of us slams a door for example, especially in anger, she says apparently equably, 'She has reeved it: and she won't be happy till it's off its hinges and then it'll be where are you. *I* don't give a hait, but she'll get the quare skelping from the boss' – and she would look darkly towards the door that led to the sitting-room. She knew that our father had never raised a hand to us in his life.

Sometimes we carry a grievance to her hoping for redress although we know it's a risky and arbitrary business since her reactions are utterly unpredictable. She may listen to the complaint with sympathy; or go over to the enemy's side, or pounce. 'Give over that rigmarole, you have me head turned, the pile of you vexing each other, and vexing me.' If a rigmarole seems to make a sense or she is in a mood for vengeance she rushes off like a whirlwind, eyes snapping, cheeks reddened, to dole out rough justice. Any faint satisfaction one feels at such an effect is speedily dissolved, in fear of retribution. But more often than not all Ellen can do is to hold out for peace, and under this system the youngest child, who shrieks with an indifference beyond us, gets what she wants simply to stop the noise. And what the ba wants is invariably what we have and want to keep.

'Will yous give over, and give it to her,' Ellen shouts. 'My head's turned and there's you, a big bad girl, taking things from her, to keep her at it, or to get her started. You don't know what end of you is up with badness.'

'It's mine. I got it.' The claims to ownership pour from our mouths.

'Give it here out of your fist.' Ellen seizes the disputed object and gives it to the baby who lapses for a while into silence while you vow once more to punish and possibly kill as soon as you can get at her.

Every day is full of excitation in Ellen's kitchen, and as the hour draws near to dinner or tea-time the atmosphere becomes taut with excitement and suppressed hysteria as she tries to co-ordinate everything in time for the men's hungry arrival from the farm and rampars and meadows. Some of the smaller children, Morgan, Sinclare or Nell, still too young to be out with the men, hindering rather than helping, would tuck themselves unobtrusively into corners before the actual climax.

The ritual lead-up starts with her ceremonial progress to the back door; tucking her arms under her bosom, swaddled in a print overall, she throws open the door and lets out a yell that rips down the air into the haggart. That fall call makes Nellie and Bess stamp their feet and Dick whinny and the men hasten to finish unloading the last of the hay on the lifter. We drop everything and converge on the kitchen, bursting through the door, mad for food. Ellen is invariably scandalized by this behaviour; she resents having to feed us at the same time as the adults, and hisses at us like a goose. But Elizabeth, who doesn't fear Ellen at all, reaches out to lift slices of whatever is already on the table. Ellen makes smacking gestures at the marauding hand, her mouth thinning, her eyes flashing. She has not much time to be vituperative; the men will soon be in the house. 'Get out of it, your gorb', she hisses, 'cocking yourself up on the men's chairs. There wasn't one of you here when I wanted you. There's none of you worth a ball of blue.' A ball of blue cost a half-penny and was used to make the wash whiter. We were quite unfazed.

The men file through the door, wash their hands at the jaw-box and dry them on the roller-towel on the back of the door. As they sit down at the tables they take off their flat caps and hang them over one knee, which they keep bent under their chairs. This gives them a curiously reverential appearance as though they are kneeling at a sacramental table. Where they push up their sleeves to wash their arms there is a white tender patch of skin, as there is above the line of their caps on their foreheads, and this new unused flesh is one of the most intimate things I have ever seen. It makes me perceive these men as people like us, children who have grown up with the same soft flesh as we under their old armoury of perpetually grimed clothes. But such awareness paradoxically only makes me shyer of them, more aware of their endurance and the carapace of years.

They all know that Ellen is walking-out or 'going with' Joe, Tamsie's brother, and some of the more daring men banter with her, asking her if there is any chance of them getting fixed up. Ellen blushes and whists them. 'The mistress'll hear you,' she says in mock dread; but it is Tamsie with his stooped shoulders and curious green eyes who stops the teasing, by his silence. He is what people call a modest man and people are careful of this modesty.

Every night Ellen slips across the Bush Hill to meet her lover, there being nowhere else to go. God knows what comfort they can have had in all weathers out over on the Bush Hill. 'Pity poor lovers, who may not do what they please with their kisses under a hedge,' wrote the Irish poet Austin Clarke; and when I read this years later I thought sadly of Ellen and her blighted love on that windy hill.

But then all love seemed fated to be blighted in Ireland, in another deadly kind of famine. Even the words used for the progression of courtship and love are diminishing and unsympathetic, and make the whole business of love and tenderness seem pathetic, ridiculous, so that the effects and states of being in love become matters for concealment. The first kindling of sexual interest, the recognition of anyone of the opposite sex as being special, is called 'having a notion of' and is regarded as a foolish state. Infatuation, or the bloom state of being-in-love, is called being astray in the head – and being astray in the head about someone is only a hound's howl away from being away in the head which means being carted off to Omagh, along with poor Lena.

There was little opportunity for overt courtship: no meeting-places for young couples; no system whereby they could get to know each other until they plighted their troth. A young man who wanted to 'go' with a girl of his fancy asked another man to put in a good word for him, and if the response was favourable they continued to meet and then to start 'going'. But often a young couple tried to keep their attachment secret – perhaps because a public liaison, however frail and new, was tantamount to a betrothal. Everyone knew that Ellen was going with Joe, but it was never openly acknowledged: they never once appeared in public together.

For twenty years Ellen dreams of getting married and having children, and as she watches her contemporaries and sisters (and she was herself one of ten children) doing both she plans in ever more detail her wedding. She has a wedding-suit made at the local tailor, the equivalent of having the banns read, but the suit hangs on the back of her door covered by a white flour bag. On the rare occasions when we enter her bedroom over the kitchen I keep my eyes averted from it. It looks to me like a pitiful integument waiting for her body. At some point Ellen began to mourn instead of to plan.

Easy and tempting perhaps now to see in her aggressive movements, that air of desperation, those battles with the ingredients of the meals she so endlessly prepared an expression of her frustrations, disappointments and unfulfilled hopes. She loves us, feeds us, cares for us, protects us, but we are not her children, and we love her and are grateful to her, and the ambivalence in loving her we resolve in later ways.

7

The harvest time is the busiest time of the year for Ellen. Some meadows are too far away for the men to come back to the house for tea, so we take it up to them wherever they are working, and Ellen starts preparing and packing up the tea even while we are still at the dinner. The men working in distant meadows are either over at Eglish, my father's other little farm down by Golloman's Point at the lough shore, or up in the interstices of the aerodrome, where farmers can still cultivate the land between the perimeters and the runways that had been theirs before it was requisitioned at the beginning of the war.

To get on to the aerodrome we drive up the tiny rutted road

which falls between two territories, that of the military aviation and the County Council, and thus is never repaired by either. It is pitted with deep holes full of that deadly petrol-stained water, and the car lurches and pitches from one hole to another while my father curses and we try to keep the tea-cans and food-baskets on a level keel. 'Bad cess to them, wouldn't you think they'd fill up one pothole,' he says as the car sinks to its axle in a new hole that has, he avers, appeared unbeknownst since he negotiated the road the very same morning.

When we get to the top of the road and on to the runway the size and smoothness of the surface seem miraculous, and so patterned with mirages that we seem to be driving into smooth sheets of water. It is a different world up there, as we leave within a space of a hundred yards the overgrown, hedge-ridden denseness of the original untouched countryside for the flatness of a prairie. Here even the biggest balers, threshers and tractors become only drowning specks on the horizon and the sky is domed like a blue glass bowl, trapping us underneath, as Ellen sometimes traps the silverfish in the scullery.

The wind-stocking fluttering to show pilots which way the wind is blowing is like a plump white arm waving across the horizon. Every time I see it I think of Excalibur being delivered to King Arthur, an image culled from the *Children's Encyclopaedia* of which we possess a complete set. We read its ten volumes with extreme selectivity, looking at the pictures (reproductions of Pre-Raphaelite paintings, Our Artists' renderings of Epic British Battles, Famous Views of Famous Cities), and reading the Encyclopaedia's staid equivalent of comic strips – educative photographs with captions underneath – and skimming through the legends and fairy stories that were meant to leaven the text. The articles were full of references to Children of Other Lands, the British Empire, and descriptions of the White Man's Burden. It would have been hard to find a less relevant or more subversive way of presenting the world to us than this middle-class English publication, with colonialism at its very core. We read it with derisory but uneasy interest. For us, half-way between Britain and Ireland, it is a missive from a world that has significance but

72

no meaning; the aerodrome is part of that outside world lying beyond, arbitrary and destructive.

The building of the aerodrome split the parish in two; its centre was blitzed and cut by black runways that look like enormous scorch marks across the surface. It did something else to the parish too. It caused the extinction of a place. The land was rolled flat, every hedge and tree cut down, every home destroyed; instead of the small undulations of hillocks, there were the regular contours of bomb-storage mounds to draw the eye. A shooting-range became the highest structure in the district, higher than the Old Cross; and, most devastating of all, there was no through road from the lower half of the parish to the upper part, and thus to the world. 'They cut the very heart out of the parish,' my father said. 'They didn't even cut it in half, they just went for the heart and planted it in the Claggan, the only village in Ardboe. There were more people living there than anywhere else, a thousand acres of good farm land was taken, thirty families evacuated, leaving the nine families in Sessiagh and the fifteen families of Farnsagh lopped off from the rest of the world.' In the Claggan every disappeared hillock and mound had had a name that told and contained the kernel of its history; and the people who knew the names, and why they were so called, were removed to another district as anonymous to them as the place they left behind had become anonymous.

There was no precedent or apparatus for dissent then, no means available to the population for objecting to compulsory removal from their homes or the requisition of their land. Perhaps there was no redress for such war-time expedients anywhere in Britain; and on the map, in the Department of Defence in far-away Stormont where the Ulster Government sat, Ardboe must have appeared as an ideal site for an aerodrome, being comparatively flat, with vast empty flying approaches from over the lough. But the aerodrome (as anyone who lived there could have told the planners in advance) is more often than not rendered inoperable because of the mist that rolls in from the lough; nearly every day we hear the aeroplane engines revving and spluttering above the clouds as they turn, abandon further attempted abortive approaches and head for the nearest aerodrome with enough visibility to land.

When at last the servicemen departed and the runways and perimeters began to crumble into friable black lumps of tarmac and the small hedges and stunted trees that had been uprooted began to grow again, straggling across the unnatural flatness, forming no boundaries, the landscape had a peculiar and terrible desolation. Even war-ravaged countryside soon returns with reoccupation and husbandry to some semblance of how it was; but the Air Ministry still leased this land and it lay and lies untended. When I walked up there on my own I felt that if I put my ear to the earth, as I did on our own undamaged ground only a few hundred yards away, I would hear only a dazed amnesiac moan. Such a fancy was pathetic fallacy in every sense. But I never walk that wounded ground without feeling that a terrible violence had been dealt to Ardboe, in one of the small unremarked, unrecorded obscenities of war.

The building of the aerodrome threw life in Lower Ardboe even more into itself than before: for the lough and its water bailiffs formed an equally effective barrier on the other side of what had become a peninsula. Our life was curiously unaffected by the technology of the aerodrome. It remained an enclosed world; and although there was radio communication for air traffic control and a complex telephone system linked the various buildings in the aerodrome, for years there was only one public call-box in the district, beside the post office a mile away, and our wireless – one of the very few – was a crystal set powered by wet batteries.

The aerodrome was reopened for a short time in the late 1950s for training English pilots. The runways and perimeters were rebuilt and the wayward hedges again uprooted, and occasionally on our way home from school we played a form of dare by dancing on the perimeter in front of the taxi-ing aeroplanes (which must have much amused the trainee pilots); although these perimeters that lie so close to our world were studded with landing-lights, electricity was still not available to the surrounding community.

Sometimes I went up on the aerodrome by myself looking for the rare nests of those birds who build in and on the ground. I knew where and how to find larks' nests, by watching them sing high in the sky and observing where they plummet; and I knew how to find the nest which peewits make in the ground among tussocks and flat earth, and knew that the female peewit remains crouched on its nest of eggs or fledglings, hoping to go unfound, until the searcher is almost on top of her; then when danger is too near to be avoided, she rises with an alarmed diversionary beating of wings, and a shrieking call, before falling back to the ground, wings trailing, limping slowly away. She seems so crippled, so injured, that any predator – fox or stoat or human – will surely follow such easy prey. Only when the predator has been lured sufficiently far from the nest will she soar into the air uninjured.

I am, of course, as profoundly moved by this natural manifestation of the maternal instinct as I am by the biblical story that the Needle reads off the Cross of the woman who yields her baby to her rival rather than have Solomon divide it. Both actions have to do with maternal love, and I find them reassuring. I am also comforted by the presence of the peewit and the larks, as they at least are continuing the contract with the earth which humans have broken. I look for the corncrake's nest too, but I never see one, nor find its nest, although I search assiduously and its hoarse rattle like a crash of vocal gears in the throat punctuates all our childish evenings.

Bringing in the tea to the men is always a memorable excursion. We do not often get a ride in the car on weekdays and hardly ever with Ellen along too; the unaccustomedness of her presence heightens our excitement and she is flushed and pleasantly irritable, her eyes clenching as she counts over the food (which she calls victuals) and the cups and mugs in the baskets. Besides the unusualness of her presence, there is also the moment of anarchy when the car turns off the tarmac and takes to the field, bumping over the ruts and stubble towards the black squares and specks that are the men and machines. The drone coming from the biggest of these shapes – the baler and thresher – rises and falls on the unblocked air like the snores of a somnolent giant. It is the same noise we hear with such heightened sensitivities on the day Elizabeth leaves home for school, but it is still unfreighted with this gaunt association on the day I remember. For instead of these aerodrome days being a sunny blur in the memory, a flickering series of days over my childhood years, they are reduced to one, a distillation corked in my head, and I have only to pull the cork of memory for the essence of that extraordinary day, the sights, smells, sounds and sensibilities, to rise around me.

Elizabeth and Eiram, Morgan and I climb into the car carefully, each of us carrying baskets of sandwiches and farls of soda bread, apples and scones, and a tin can of hot tea. Since it is nearing the evening of the long harvest day my father decides he will bring each of the men a bottle of stout to drink at the heel of the day. Ellen takes off the flowered cross-over apron that holds her body in its accustomed contours, and that action too reveals her in a different light; she looks unfamiliar out of the overall. Carrying the biggest basket she gets into the front passenger-seat of the car and we drive to the pub where my father leaps out, leaving the handbrake on and the engine running – since it is often a job with a starting handle to start it. We know that our father has gone in to pick up the Guinness for the men and won't be long, but Ellen climbs out to wait; she mistrusts engines of any kind and does not like to be alone with this one throbbing away with no one at the controls.

The time, however, our father is away for longer than usual and after a while Elizabeth puts her basket of sandwiches on the floor, clambers into the driver's seat, grasps the steering wheel, lets off the handbrake and away we go. The car rolls down the Brae Hill, past Biddy's house, her eyes glittering from the darkness of her doorway, past the well where Lena seeks watery nirvana, past John-Joe Campbell rocking himself on his hunkers at the end of his loaning, and as unmoved by the sight of three small children being driven at some speed by one only marginally bigger as he is by any other event except Lena on my trike, past Lodelley the best fisherman on the lough, puffing on his bicycle on his way to his boat, and towards the big ivy-covered tree whose roots spreading under the road have caused the tarmac to rupture and the tar to gather in little pools of wicked liquid that Franky O'Neill smears on his fingers and chases us with. As we career faster and faster towards the tree, Morgan puts her bucket of food gently onto the floor, leans over and hauls on the handbrake with both hands. The car slows down and rolls gently into the tree, rather than crashing into it. Morgan's hands fold slowly back in her lap.

The tea that has slopped out from under the lid of the tin as we rolled along is burning my thigh. Elizabeth's hands are still holding the steering-wheel. Behind us we can hear Ellen and my father shouting as they run.

We stay frozen behind the glass and then the door opens. My father leans in and lifts out Elizabeth, whitefaced, from behind the wheel, and we scramble out from the back.

'Yous all could have been kilt,' Ellen screams. She crosses herself and scowls and won't look straight at us in case we are not all right.

'Jaysus, Mary and Joseph, what'll she be up to next, the divil's in her as big as a goat,' she says to my father who kneels beside the white-faced Elizabeth.

'You've got a fright', he says, 'and gave us one too.' He holds her tight and we stand whey-faced behind him. He reverses the car out of the tree and we all get in again. No one says anything to Morgan about her presence of mind.

Ellen, still trembling and vibrating, turns round from time to time to check on us and what boldness we might be up to and sees the stain on my dress. 'She'll have it all spilt afore she gets there,' she says to no one in particular. The excitement of the car journey, our misadventure, the prospect of tea with the men, all make her skin dark with nervous excitement. As we climb out of the car for the second time Eiram's legs, with their strong-hollowed backs to the knees, the tense calves, run far ahead outstepping Elizabeth's and Morgan's and mine. The men have seen us coming from a long way off and they switch off the machines so the noise is juddering to a halt by the time we reach them. Ellen spreads the oilcloth on the stubble underneath the shadow of the thresher – there is no natural shade here, since all the trees and hedges have been cleared for visibility between runways – and the men swing down over the sides or jump from the top of the thresher. Those who have been tossing the hay or corn up, stick their pitchforks into the ground. The atmosphere is tense with thirst.

Some of the men lie down immediately, stretching out and resting on one elbow, while others kneel on one knee hanging their caps on the other as they do in the kitchen, and I see again that white flesh above the rolled-up sleeves of their shirts as they reach for the cheese and sandwiches and baps. As they eat they relax, and by the end of the meal even those who began kneeling on the one knee have sunk on to the ground and are sprawled, inhaling their cigarette smoke. There is one basket that hasn't been unpacked – the one with the bottles of stout in it. They are for when the men finish work. If they were to drink it now, in the heat of the sun, they would become heavy and drowsy, hardly fit to waddle, as Ellen says briskly.

Everyone suddenly discusses whether or not the weather will hold until the harvest is finished. What makes them uneasy is that the martins and swallows are beginning to fly low over the ground – a sign of impending rain. It seems hard to believe, in this golden haze. One of the men suddenly, to his own and everyone else's surprise, quotes a line of poetry:

Lo, low over the fields, the swallow wings.

He looks abashed at this rush of blood to the head and another man staring slyly at my father says, 'I don't care if they're walking it, I'm leaving at six.' Everyone laughs but is somewhat shocked, for when the weather is fine they work till it is dark whatever the hour. Our father, lying with his dark head propped in his hand, finishes the verse:

. . . the cricket too, how sharp it sings,
Puss on the hearth with velvet paws
Sits purring o'er her whiskered jaws.

There is a silence, and a collective gesture towards some vanished schoolroom, and the shadows lengthen at the far edges of the aerodrome.

The blue dome darkens. Ellen gathers up the plates and cups and packs them into the basket. She shakes out the tablecloth and the men put out their cigarettes, some carefully pinching them at the ends and putting them behind their ears to finish later, others grinding them into the stubble. They rise slowly, heavily, and go

78

back to their idle machines. The tractors crash into life, the fan-belts begin to spin, the grain pours through wooden spouts into jute bags attached below them which grow as fat as Nellie's rump within minutes. We thrust our hands into the golden spill, and turn them round and round as though washing them in a golden downpour, as if summer could solidify its liquid essence as winter can in snow and hail.

Our father examines the grain, running his hands through it in a different manner, rubbing individual grains between his fingers. He rarely works in the fields – only when one of the men is away or is taken ill – and this is a rare occurrence. He always wears a suit and sometimes a large black leather coat and trilby hat, and when he is lying down on the stubble, languid but full of a tensile energy, he looks to me like the young Elizabethan gallant in the Isaac Oliver reproduction in one of the encyclopaedias at home, although that young beauty is dressed in elaborate and embroidered costume.

I love this image deeply. The young man lying on the grass among the trees, so indolent and yet alert, his dark eyes intently gazing out of the picture full of an absolute and serene confidence, his shock of black curly hair springing from his high white forehead, his head resting lightly on the hand emerging from the lacy frills of his blue silk lace-goffered costume. He seems courtesy and grace itself, the parfait knight of the old stories in the loft, and strapped on his left arm is a shield – not an instrument of war but a lovely toy, inscribed with the legend 'magica sympathia'. I knew were he ever to utter he would speak in the voice of my father who was magic and sympathy itself.

Once walking home from school I saw my gallant father ploughing with the two horses, Nellie and Bess. I was astonished, and watched in a trance as the share cleaved the ground, leaving a red rib of earth undulating behind. I heard the low clicking noises in his throat with which he coaxed and lured the huge mares to back up and move sideways and turn around in their own space, and these noises, that image, his arms outstretched and strained grasping the handles, the coulter breaking the earth upwards, slid into my heart alongside Eiram at the post office and Morgan, at night, kneeling to say her prayers.

8

Our father is physically a very beautiful man and by far the most powerful figure in our lives, a figure who outranks every other adult within our sphere for years, as fathers do. But added to the natural power and attraction which by position and kinship he must already possess for his children, he has other attributes that make him remarkable. His charm is a most winning means to an end, the end being to please the other person, although he never bothers to beguile for the sake of self-interest, and has no time for those he dislikes or despises. We feel, jealously, that perhaps he has too much time for others. He suffers fools gladly, and is ever ready to find humour in a foible, to exploit it for his own amusement and as the basis for the anecdotes that are his only form of formal conversation.

If he dislikes or distrusts someone he treats them with a coldness that seems to us astonishing and alarming; and those thus treated appear like the lost souls of limbo cast into the exterior darkness and suffering the worst punishment of all, the withdrawal of light. He is one of the few adults who never seem to feel the need to vex our spirits through some incurable itch of their own sick hearts, and sometimes I feel we live our lives as though anticipating and pining his loss, although he rarely leaves home for any length of time. This feeling is something more than the normal childish fear of the withdrawal or disappearance of parental love for reasons of one's own inadequacy. We fear it because there is something haunted or unattainable about him, as though he perpetually seeks for something he lost in some distant time beyond us. Even when he is laughing his eyes seem to have a proximity to pain. Perhaps this is the interpretation that all anxious children put on their parents' secret expressions.

His beautiful face, which would have been dashingly handsome – as was his brother's – had he not suffered a broken nose during a boxing bout at school and which is, in repose, forlorn, lights up when he is telling those endless anecdotes, like a match flaring in a dark room. He has a joyous and childlike quality, and something else, something gorgeous in its true meaning, an exoticism in his character which is startling in that district of plain people; and that is why, I later realize, he reminds me of the Elizabethan gallant in his delicious finery. I also realize, much later, that he is a gambler.

Our father is memorable both in himself and in his antecedents. The neighbours and Tamsie tell us stories about him as a child: how beautiful he was, and how bad; a boy who threw cats down the well, who took boats out on the lough by himself; a tumble of beautiful curls appearing at a small upstairs lavatory window in response to an alarmed cry from the yard below. 'Your parents and brother have met up with an accident in the trap', a man shouted up to him, 'all couped in a ditch on the road to Cookstown and for all we know all kilt.'

'Good enough,' my then four-year-old father is reputed to have called back, smiling winsomely. 'Then I'll get the prog.' I looked up prog later: an old English word meaning provender.

There are four children in his immediate family – an unusually small number for Ireland in those days – and they are famous for their beauty. We can see why when we look at those old photographs in the albums in the house and in the loft. In the one we know best and look at most often, taken outside the front door of that grand new house built by his father, and framed in the hall, the four children are standing around the rising young politician Eammon de Valera, who is later condemned to death for his part in the Easter Rising of 1916 and who alone of those famous insurgents escapes execution, because he was born in the United States. He escaped from prison in England and became President of the Dail, the newly formed and illegal Assembly of Ireland.

The two men, he and my grandfather, his Northern agent, one as tall as the other, dressed exactly alike, stand glowering at the camera. The four children are grave and formal, the girls in lacy white dresses, the two boys, my father and uncle, in knicker-bockers and black stockings. All have the high foreheads, burnished hair, gleaming waxy skin, and enormous eyes that Elizabeth and Sinclare have inherited. His four children are an important part of our grandfather's ambition, part of his endless fight against the creep of the place he was born in.

Alone of all the children in the district, they go to boarding-school, and on to further education, except for my father who refuses to stay at the school, where he has been systematically terrorized by a sadistic and brutal priest. He comes home halfway through his school career, refuses further education, refuses to venture out beyond the territory he has marked out as a child.

His eldest brother, whom he reverés, becomes a doctor, which although an ordinary enough achievement in other parts of the western world is, given the defeating geographical, political and social isolation in which he lives, and the crippling lack of expecta-tion, an enormous feat. The Doctor, as he is called, is the only man from the district to have moved into the professional classes until the mid-1960s when that world began to open out. His two sisters, too, went to university and then abroad, and my father mourns their disappearance all his life, although they often return home for family reunions. For him, I think, childhood remains the only real place and all else is a banishment. He tells us fragments of his life with an utter simplicity, revealing what has happened, laying it out, and giving glimpses of times that were so hard that we seem by comparison to be living in luxury.

'It was during the Depression, the black Thirties', he says, 'and if the rest of the world was poor then this country here was poorer. There wasn't any money to be had in the countryside. Not a brass farthing. And I had a grey racing bike. I loved that bike, it was small, very fast. We had grown potatoes and it was a great year. We lifted twenty-seven tons of potatoes, but couldn't sell them. There was nobody to buy them. There were piles of potatoes rotting all over the countryside. I heard of a man in Cookstown who was buying potatoes and I got on the bicycle and I rode into the town like the wind, and when I got there I found the man and told him I had potatoes for sale and they were good ones. And they *were*. The best. And he said "I'll give you a pound a ton." A pound a ton.' In his voice we heard again the pain of that moment.

'I said to the man, "I can't sell you them till I tell my father and mother. Will you wait till I go home and ask them?" It was a twelve-mile journey, each way. "I will not," he said. "Take it or leave it. Will you sell or will you not?" and I said, "I will."

82

And I went home with £27 for twenty-seven tons. Fields and fields of crops. All we had. But I was better off than some. For I met a man with a pony and a cart full of potatoes. And he said he had gone to an old flaxhole and had started to tip the potatoes into the hole. When a farmer came running out of the house and shouted at him, "Move on, be at your business," it turned out that he wanted the flaxhole for his own potatoes. It was the only way to get rid of them.'

The story for anyone who knows, however cursorily, Ireland's history, reverberates with wails and echoes. Potatoes are rooted not only in the soil of Ireland but in its sorry legend.

My father's voice when he is talking to us takes on a certain intimate tone; in this voice he composes long complicated stories, each an odd mixture of fantasy and reality, whose setting is often a fairyland guarded by a small wooden gate which lies below Biddy's Brae. So palpable and probable does he make this Ultima Thule that I never walk down the Brae Hill, or, more likely, run down it the quicker to get past Biddy and her imprecations towards Campbell's loaning and John-Joe on his hunkers but that I don't look covertly, hopefully, for that enchanted entrance glinting among the hawthorns.

Yet every story he tells holds in it too a morsel of the pain of his country. The pain finds its most poignant expression in the songs that, terribly out of tune, he sings to us at night. We are moved by his voice, by its cracked timbres, its unconcealed sensual sadness, as though he is mourning having to leave his home to become another Irish exile, although he has never strayed or wandered. That voice, off-key and out of tune, also contains nostalgia for a past that, as we recognize from our beginnings, remains in many ways his present.

He is not a good singer, unlike most of the men of the district, who sing in voluptuously sad voices as a natural expression of their feelings. They sing two kinds of songs, both handed down orally over generations: ballads known as 'come-all-yees', because they start with the words 'Come all ye lads and lassies'; and laments, long threnodies of grief and exile, banishments, hunger, disease and death and hopeless rebellions, the sad ways of our Irish life, elegies for those who emigrated and dirges for those who stayed behind. There is, though, an element of celebration in the songs, acknowledgement of endurance and survival; and in the words, in their utterance and in the music there is, too, that compassion – the use of the imagination to encompass the condition of others – that is so characteristic of many of the Irish.

Life is lamented in these songs: it is the only appreciation of beauty we see and hear – the apprehension of sorrow, the waste of love, the wastage of people. Through these songs we learn our history. There is no other way to learn it – certainly not at school where Irish history is a subversive subject; and as we learn, it becomes literally a sob story, as indeed it is. There is the squeeze of pain in every episode, and although people sometimes say that the Irish are great lickers of wounds, they have had many to lick.

Perhaps no other nation is more ready to cry, to be more borne down by the sadnesses inherent in human existence. The great national monuments of Ireland are dead heroes – preferably those who died young, unfulfilled and beautiful, leaving legend and inspiration behind, but rarely tangible improvements in the lot of those they inspired; and if such a hero left a young girl bereft, *intacta* and keening behind him, so much the better for a sad song. Many of these songs have layers of special connections and meanings for us – *Slieve Gallion Brae* for example, one of the most beautiful of the ballads regularly sung in the evening in my father's little pub, is about a mountain that lies on the horizon only ten miles away. We know its every contour.

'It was a characteristic much noted by officials and previous settlers of wherever the Irish fled to, that they, above all other nations, clung to their memories of their lost land,' wrote an historian; and listening to these songs, we know with certitude that these emigrants felt Ireland as a living part of them which had been wrenched away. As a man whose leg has been amputated feels a phantom nerve twitching in the night, so Ireland shivers at the extremities, and the loss in the song is matched by the loss of those who are left behind. There is often apparent around us a wild extravagance of grief, as though it is the only possible or permissible show of emotion; and when my father evinces this in his singing, our world is revealed in its reality as a place of grief and exile.

Our prayers and rituals which we recite daily deliver the same lesson – that we live in a vale of tears, a place of pain, a stopping on the road to somewhere else, where once we had been whole. We pray, 'Hail Holy Queen. Mother of Mercy, Hail our life, our sweetness and our hope. To You do we cry poor, poor banished children of Eve. To You do we send up our sighs, mourning and weeping in this valley of tears, and as we chant our lives become tainted with forlornness.'

Years later on her wedding day Eiram sang *Slieve Gallion Brae* and any stranger not aware of how thin the membrane is between grief and joy in Irish celebrations might have considered it somewhat inappropriate. My sister's new husband noted how his bride's song shivered the day, noted too that grief which so often marks my father's face, and names these things in a poem, written years after the event:

I am afraid
Sound has stopped in the day,
And the images reel over
And over. Why all those tears,

The wild grief on his face
Outside the taxi? The sap
Of mourning rises
In our waving guests

You sing behind the tall cake
Like a deserted bride
Who persists, demented
And goes through the ritual

When I went to the gents
There was a skewered heart
And a legend of love. Let me
Sleep on your breast to the airport.*

For years I think we all believed that our incipient melancholia came to us direct from our father, and that for us his way of living, of celebrating and of lamenting was not just a case of his calling back his yesterday, but also of calling back our tomorrows;

* Seamus Heaney.

he seemed able to turn over the leaves of our future and embed in them, just under the surface, a dolorous watermark.

It is only when we are grown up we realize that it is a human longing for the past to be rescued or redeemed, and that our predilection towards what Cardinal Newman called 'that ripping up of old griefs, and the venturing again upon the *infandum dolorem* of years in which the stars of this lower heaven were, one by one, going out' was not just a legacy but belonged newly to each one of us.

9

In one direction the aerodrome makes an enormous boundary to our dominions; in the other the lough is our limit. But the aerodrome is alien and forbidden, while the lough lures us with every wave that laps against the shore-line. We go there almost every day, summer and winter, when we are not at school, or after school, spending hours in the graveyard above or the shore below.

In the summer, the whole of the lough shore is so banded by midges that to get to the water we have to drill a space through their fluctuating galaxies, which rise and fall in an electric intensity all along the shore and above the water, so it looks as though a dark ectoplasmic veil is suspended along its edges. The midges hardly bother us, we have inhaled them since birth and become immune; we move through them unconcerned, blinking them away and exhaling them, although visitors collide with the tiny green living filaments in their thousands and retreat, blind and coughing, their eyes streaming, their clothes fretted suddenly black with a floating living spume.

High spirals of connected insects form and rise along the shore, long shivering conglomerations twisting and snaking in the air like plumes of dark smoke among the more loosely connected larger swarms. It makes the lough shore shimmer like a *pointilliste* painting. The midges thin out as the ground rises, so most visitors return to or remain up in the graveyard. When we are up there in the graveyard the water below seems an impossible element, unavailably far away; an extraordinary transformation comes over us whenever we overcome that quivering passionate reluctance and go down to the shore.

We are instinctively apprehensive of the water. In the haggarts and meadows, in the byres and stables and lofts, when we are deep in vegetation, or chasing butterflies, picking sorrel and wild raspberries, strawberries and blackberries, looking for nests or walking across the Fallow Field to Matty's Hill, skirting the fairy tree, we are so much a part of the earth's growing things that we feel like grain, and hardly brush away the seeds of grass or hay that cling to the corners of our mouths, so much are they a part of our own texture.

At these times water is a foreign and threatening element – threatening, since it can soak and rot grain and crop, and is only necessary, drop by drop, to sustain our existence. We puddle and splash in liquid when the earth has tempered or accommodated it in the keshes around the meadow, in the glaucous flaxholes where the frog-spawn slithers between our fingers, or in the deep muddy ditches between fields and under hedges where we wade on the quest for strawberries and bird's nests.

Ellen is not best pleased when we return home after having been communing with nature in this way. 'In clabber to your lugs', she says, 'and worsen pigs, for they *have* to be in it, and there's no having on you, only wanting to puddle in muck and glaur. Don't be coming into *this* kitchen with them clabbery feet.' One day I so far forgot myself as to paddle across the kitchen in my muddy gum-boots to get to the tea-table the earlier. Ellen came in from the scullery and, seeing the trail, was confounded. Then she gave voice: 'Ah, Sweet Jaysus.' Her voice soared. 'She's in glaur to the oxters on me nice clean floor.' She unfroze and was on me like a whirlwind and I was out of the door again, dazed, before I knew what had hit me. '*Ellen* hit you,' Nell said with satisfaction. In the declension of earthiness, mould is relatively clean and thin, clabber is thick and dirty, and glaur is the ultimate – an oozing heavy wetness that clings to all the many extremities of child and beast, and glaur is what Ellen hates, and we love. A mixture of earth and water, with earth winning.

Yet as soon as we get near the shore and smell the water we become as intent on it as otters or mermaids, amphibious creatures, incapable of living without it, and craving it. Yet still we are afraid of the lough. It is a big hostile creature. Although we have taught ourselves to swim we always keep within our depth, threshing our arms to convince ourselves we are doing breaststroke, pulling ourselves along from boulder to boulder. The water, being fresh water, is not buoyant, and always very cold. When we climb out again, edging over the sharp stones like turtles in our old swimsuits or knickers and vests, we are covered in goose-pimples which take a long time to disappear.

The silvery expanse of the lough, besides being a unique playground, also delivers grand analogies about our hopes, our aspirations, the trammels of our existence. We are not slow to gloat on symbols. It looks so boundless from our ground level, but is landlocked in its hollow glacial plain. It is traversed by the river Bann, which enters it at Maghery at the top of the lough and flows out towards the sea at Toome on the other side, where the eel fisheries are and where King, the water bailiff, has his headquarters. Sometimes looking down from the graveyard I think I can discern the darker heavier current of the river sliding through the stiller waters of the lough, in an exclusive lambent channel.

There are endless diversions along the shore and we usually have the whole place to ourselves. We pick the pliable green and glossy rushes which grow out of the water and practise making the St Brigid's Crosses that are brought to the church on St Brigid's Day, 2 February, to be blessed by the priest. They hang behind a holy picture in every kitchen in the parish for the rest of the year, drying from their frail new greenness to a pale crackly brown. The more dextrous among us can weave intricate variations into the basic designs. The little crosses have no great significance for us; only years later do we realize that they are important secret artefacts of what was for years a deprived and forbidden faith, whose believers had to make its implements and icons how and as they could.

We pick the pods of the yellow iris and wriggle our hands in the eel-cages, and if the boats are moored in their little dug-out quays we clamber in and out, fiddling with the oars and pretending we are actually out on the waters. We constantly yearn for the miracle to happen, for the fishermen suddenly to ask us to come out with them to set or lift their lines; and this does occasionally happen, just often enough for us to continuously carry on our subtle negotiations, with superstition and hope. Occasionally, and at arbitrary intervals, we are given to understand that if the weather remains fine and if we present ourselves at dawn by the boats, the fishermen will not refuse us. Having extracted this osmotic agreement from them we then have to get our parents to agree to the dawn outing, and with various caveats and strictures they generally do. Only Ellen prophesies disaster, loss and calamity, and peers gloomily, but with relish, into the tea-leaves at the bottom of her cup and spies sea-changes and shipwrecks and white bones. There is a legend that a city lies buried under the waves, and she sees us lying among its round towers.

There are many practical reasons for us not being allowed out in the boats more often, and they are ceaselessly advanced. We would only be a hindrance to the fishermen; they start early at dawn and finish late; we are at school a good deal of the fishing season; and of course few workers want children with them in their daily work. But there is another and more potent reason for the fishermen's reluctance to have us along, and this is the widespread belief that the lough claims one victim every year. The fishermen do not try to avert the possibility of being the single annual victim by learning to swim. 'We'll be drowned all the quicker,' they say, when questioned as to why they don't learn, and although the questioners may postulate that since the lough is usually calm, if a fisherman learns only to float he will surely be rescued, they will have none of it. They believe that the lough needs and claims that one victim, and if the mark is on you, there is little use in learning to swim since it will simply prolong the hopeless struggle. They do not like bringing us, new young bait, on to its surface. It is as though they were afraid of exciting the lough's avid curiosity. (Years and years later, when Joe Corrigan, one of the Needle's sons, the inheritor of the original two-bedroomed council house in which ten of his brothers and sisters had been reared, has a bathroom installed under a home improvement scheme, he is asked if he has actually taken a bath in his shiny new porcelain tub. He starts back in feigned alarm. 'Jaysus', he says, 'I've hardly stuck it out on the lough for nigh on forty years to be drownded in me own front room.')

Day after day we longingly watch the boats moving out across the waters, the noise of their engines getting fainter until it disappears completely and only the reverberations remain, and the odd disturbed ripple, and the silence hangs full of our unspoken disappointment. But the occasional days when we do manage to get out with the fishermen are times of such intense concentration and happiness that we are transported, not out of ourselves but into ourselves. We are utterly alone except for each other, but at such times sisters are part of your own soul. We have risen in the unaccustomed half-light of the dawn and crept down the stairs and out through the front door into a world that looks astonishingly different because we are the first to inhabit it. We break the seal on the dew and move silently down the road which lies timid in its untrodden light. The wild roses are pale against the dark green of the hedges. The graveyard is shadow and mystery, its denseness pricked by the gleam of the pale trumpets of woodbine that weave and twine about the hedges. The silence is immense.

Any stranger would surely notice the slap and sough and hiss of the lough, but for us that sound is not noise but part of the quietness. The faintest trace of a spume of mist clings to the rushes, and on a fair morning the thorn-trees creak, the lapwings call, and the whole shore has an extraordinary anticipatory paleness. Everything is leached of colour. The dark heaviness of the graveyard lies high above; here below, on the shore, the greens, yellows, brackens, browns, are still within the gift of the light that hangs, tantalizing, just above the blanched greedy surfaces of rushes, stones and water. You feel you could creep under the arriving colour as though under the fringe of an almost transparent curtain, your back just brushing it so that the air and sky will sway and ripple up to the stratosphere. Eiram's skin has a stretched translucence, Morgan's eyes are glittering and Elizabeth's hair has sucked in any colour there is, the browns and golds loose in the transparent morning.

I never see so clearly again as in those glimmering mornings by the lough shore the striking force of light, yet this striking is never audacious. The light does not penetrate like the strong sun of hotter places, but hesitates over surfaces, flickering across outlines, illuminating a whitewashed wall, the edge of a boulder, or spilling over in a dazzling accident as it collides with an angled open window at the Coyles' house. As we watch that trembling light moving towards the water's edge and meeting the water in a marvellous condensation among the fringes of grass and rushes and little brown boulders, and these expanding into spangled glittering movement, a dance between water and air, we crave to get into the middle of what is happening.

We time our impatience well. The fishermen come silently down the path that winds around the base of the Point, balancing their wedge-shaped wooden trays full of neatly coiled mounds of lines with one hand, carrying tin cans of worms or tea in the other. When they come round the sloe-bushes and see us there, mute, tense, anticipatory, they begin to laugh. 'How did you get your-selves up out of your beds at this hour?' asks Joe, Tamsie's brother. 'For the Devlins was always great sleepers.' This, we know, is a mannerly way of saying we couldn't be roused. 'Maybe Ellen roused them,' Frank, the first fisherman, says slyly. They pull on their glazers, help us clamber over the side of the boat and push off from the little dug-out cleft of a quay with their long poles. We glide past the deep water marker – a tin can on a pole perched on a rough pyramid of rocks – and once past it the men start the engine. These engines are taken out of old cars and fitted almost casually and with an elementary adaption system into boats whose designs have remained unchanged over the centuries, and which have always been built by the Coney family who live a few miles further up the lough shore. The Coneys are famous for their musicality and their general artistry.

Soon the only land mass visible, except for the vague low bulk of the shoreline, is Ram's Island, with its romantic unfulfilled attractions, and legends of how men had walked to the Island when ice had frozen over the lough, or how fishermen had had to spend the night there when caught in a sudden storm, or in hiding from King, the water bailiff. But these apocalyptic events never seem to happen in our timid times and we know nothing of sudden storms and acres of ice. Our storms are long heralded by lowering clouds and bitter winds that shake the sally trees into flurries of movement and by the sudden unaccustomed loudness in the south of the lough. Such storms are called Black Blowings.

When I am out in the boat I feel as though the lough is alive, an enormous sibilant creature across whose undulating skin we creep like tolerated parasites hoping not to disturb it. The main crop of the lough are eels that are caught with lines hundreds of yards long, fixed with hooks tied on at intervals, weighted with stones and marked with coloured corks; as the boat moves forward in a low spluttering gear, Frank plays the line out, impaling a worm on each regularly spaced hook. Soon a bunting of cork-markers bobbing on the water floats behind the boat.

Lifting the lines for the catch is a more complex affair. As they are pulled up out of the heavy green water, the eels on their hooks, flipping, jerking in spasms of what I supposed and suppose still to be acute pain, hold a deep appalling fascination for us, crouched in the stern of the boat, quiet, fatalistic and almost mesmerized. The eels are so alive as they die, twisting frantically, looping and coiling, trying to get clear of the hook impaled in their throats. I see the meaning of a throe. The fishermen get them clear quick enough. With a casual jerk they rip the hook out of the soft gullets and throw them into the half-filled barrel of water next to us, where they slither in and out of themselves in an endless living uncoagulated skein of flesh and lubricating slime so thick and gummy that after you have handled them you have to pull the slime in long strips from off your fingers.

When we finally chug into the dug-out quay the eels are tipped like a load of molten lead into old wood and wire tanks submerged in water, from where they are collected by the local fish merchant, operating illegally, and sent to Billingsgate fish market in London. It takes us some time to find our land-legs again, and we stagger about hesitantly, reluctant to recover our land personas. We are always given eels to take home whether we have been out on the lough or not, and salmon-trout and perch, and a kind of tench called a grunt, which is generally regarded as being too bony and tasteless to bother with; but we love them, to Joe's and Frank's wonderment. 'They're only rubbidgy bones,' Joe says as he gives us a bucketful to bring home. 'Only good for throwing back in the lough.' (Years later both fish become sought-after delicacies; because of the high prices paid now for pollen and tench and bream in London and Holland, the fishermen make a great deal of money from these previously despised fish.)

There is little home trade for eels or any other fish from the lough. They are all sent for export. The idea of fish is too bound up with religion, with fasting and abstinence, for it to be a popular basic food, and it is only on Fridays that families outside the immediate vicinity of the lough eat fish at all.

Later on when we follow Elizabeth to boarding-school we discover that our peers look on eels as they look on reptiles, as slimy and repulsive; and the very word is accompanied by a little emotive genteel shudder the better to show sensibility. We learn to conceal our liking for eels in order to show the same gentility, and to meet the specifications of our peers. But while we are young and untutored in such sophisticated responses we take considerable pleasure in eliciting that little shudder from visitors who have come to look at the Cross. We watch closely as they stare at the eels slithering around in an enamel bucket at their feet, undulating in phallic silver and pewter lengths up the sides and, with a bit of luck, out towards them.

I learn early on to clean and skin eels, and this causes positive tremors among onlookers. I kneel in the coarse sand and soil beside the bucket of eels, coat my fingers in sand, and plunge my hand into the writhing bodies, catch one tightly. The eel's slipperiness is negated by the friction of the sand, and it is solid in my grasp. I hit its head on a stone, and using a penknife from a fisherman turn its dangling silver belly and slit its throat, slicing through flesh and bone until the almost severed head lolls backwards, revealing a narrow gleaming glint of backbone. Then I slit down the dangling silver length of the belly and, pushing a sandy thumb into the new white bloodless slit, pull the head sharply down from its dark glistening integument like a frail sea-fruit. The peeled pewter-coloured sheaths lie wrinkled, detumescent, and I watch the faces of the onlookers with sly pleasure. 'She's not soft,' Frank says, watching me with somewhat the same expression.

Every time I pick up an eel or even see one, the name Sargasso Sea reverberates in my mind: it has a wonderfully exotic sound. Our grandfather had often told us about the extraordinary journey that eels make to get to Lough Neagh, to end up at the end of our hooks – I thought he must be making it up at first. They are spawned in the Sargasso Sea over three thousand miles away, between Bermuda and Puerto Rico, and are carried by the Gulf Stream towards Europe; the young eels are called elvers at this stage. They head for the opening of the river Bann upstream to the lough, where they remain for over ten years, maturing from brown to silver. After ten years their digestive organs start to disintegrate and they begin the journey back to their birthplace to spawn and die.

Since time immemorial, fishermen have fished the lough – the easiest way was to place nets across the only exit to the sea at the Bann opening, and to take what was netted of the massive silver harvest; but at all times, no matter how many nets or barriers were placed over the exit of the river from the lough, there was always an open passage left for the eels, called the Queen's Gap.

All this though – the whole of the Toome opening – belonged to a London-based company, as did all the fishing rights over the lough, gained originally by chicanery and corruption in the sixteenth century. The whole question of the right to fish on the lough burns holes in the fishermen's thoughts, and the battle for those rights is meshed into our background and helps to form our apprehension of the adult and official ways of the world. No one is allowed to fish without a licence, but licences are hard to get and, even when issued, are hedged with restrictions and stipulations, including one that the licensee must sell his catch to the consortium at prices lower than those on the open market. Besides the financial disadvantages, there were powerful psychological and social and cultural barriers against men applying for licences. The lough is their home ground, and to pay for a licence to fish it besides being a violent act to their own psyches would have seemed a betrayal of their fellows; the proper mistrust of the fishermen for all officialdom is so ingrained that the idea of seeking and gaining permission to earn a living for something considered a birthright is anathema and in direct conflict with their Republican and territorial instincts.

The fishermen catch brown or immature eels in what amounts more to a cull than a harvest. In their wooden boats lying so small and low in the water they seem an intrinsic part of the natural ecological system, negotiating a daily bargain with the lough and the fish and working to the extremes of their strength; but while we are growing up no one we know has a licence and the everyday occupation of fishing is fraught with excitement for us, and harassment, frustration and annoyance for the men trying to earn a living in a place where there is no other form of work, and where they and their forbears have always lived.

The chief water bailiff is called King, which for some time we thought was a grand and symbolic title but was in fact his surname. He patrols the lough from Toome in a long grey speed-boat, and whenever the fishermen are out a watchman leans on an indented tombstone at the top of the church point with his spy-glasses trained on Toome Harbour waiting for the first sign of his boat. If it comes nosing out a bonfire is immediately lit, and as the smoke rises, its casual signals containing such an urgent message, watchers on less prominent look-outs light other fires around the shore. As soon as they see the smoke, the men in the boats abandon their lines and head for the sanctuary of the shore. King, of course, has seen the smoke too and makes for the boats farthest away from the shore. If he catches them the fishermen have to appear in court where they are fined and their tackle is confiscated.

Sometimes, perhaps calculating that the boats will make it to the sanctuary before he can reach them, King goes straight to the abandoned lines with their bobbing cork markers. The watching fishermen curse, and we tremble with excitement as they see their lines so painstakingly made, so laboriously set, being hauled in by the bailiff.

'Bad cess to him, and his breed, seed and generation, wouldn't he give you the scunder looking at him,' the Needle's fourth son Willy says as he watches King's boat move in to where he had laid his line, and sees the bailiff hooking his line with its hundreds of hooks and its weights of carefully graded stones gathered from the lough's edge, and the cork markers he has whittled into shape, and drop it with the catch into the big boat's scuttle. All the time we are out on the lough, we each of us know that our sisters with us are half-hoping, half-fearing, that King will come on the lough and that we will see – and each one of us wants desperately to be the first one to see – the warning smoke from the beacon at the Cross; the idea of the chase, the anticipation is always there, but it never happens while we are out. It happens too often to others.

My father had once happened on the court hearing of the summons against Packy Maggan who had been caught as he tried to salvage his line; he defied King often and thus had been caught before, and lived in a ferment of rage about bailiffs and all forms of the law. Packy was a menacingly memorable man, six foot two in a parish of small men, and had hair shaven so closely that the grey skin showed through. He wore hand-made frame shoes and lived in a two-roomed cabin by himself, and there is a legend among us that he has not washed for fifty years. Certainly his buckskin trousers are moulded to him through a lubricating mixture of oil and dirt like a second skin, and at any given opportunity, if he finds himself with us on the road or at the shore and there are no adults around, he laboriously unbuttons his greasy flies. We wisely keep this peccadillo to ourselves and avoid him as much as possible.

My father with his selective sense of humour relishes watching pretension in action and enjoys witnessing and hearing the bewilderment and confusion of those in authority from outside our parish boundaries as they try to deal rationally with the mild anarchy within. He describes these cultural clashes and misunderstandings with sly and rancorous delectation.

'Packy came into the court room and immediately saw me at the back of the room. He gave me a big black wink and I had to look away and pretend I hadn't seen him for fear I would laugh and be put out for contempt of court; the clerk of the court said:

' "Is Packy Maggan in court?"

'There was no answer, and he said again, "Is Packy Maggan in court?"

' "Don't you know well I'm in court?" Packy suddenly shouted furiously. "Are yous all blind?"

' "Are you Packy Maggan?" the clerk said.

' "I am surely," Packy said. "You know that rightly. Wasn't it you's brought me here?"

'The clerk pointed at Packy and said to the bailiff, "Do you know this man?"

' "I have known him for thirty-five years or thereabouts," he said.

' "I niver knowed you," Packy said, staring at him with an utter lack of recognition. "I never seen him between the two eyes." King, unmoved, stared back. "Nor you niver knowed me. He's telling a parjured."

' "Silence," the clerk said.

' "What is a parjured?" the magistrate enquired.

' "Perjury," the clerk whispered.

'The magistrate looked shocked and began to reprimand Packy; and then seeing how pointless was such a reprimand, directed the court to proceed. Sentence was pronounced, Packy found guilty, fined, and ordered to forfeit all equipment found in his boat. He was further warned against making serious allegations against anyone in court, at which he protested loudly. "It's ugly ugly law," he shouted, and was led off muttering.'

Afterwards my father, with certain mischievous intent, questioned him. '*Did* you know the bailiff, Packy?'

'Ah, Sweet Jesus', Packy said, spitting into the corner, 'sure you know rightly that I knowed him like a begging ass.'

About the same time as we were roaming the lough shore, a young man named Pat Duffy who lived some ten miles further up the shore, but deeper inland, was also drawn to the water: he too watched the fishermen race for the shore, watched their harassment by the water bailiffs. And when he became a lawyer he brilliantly fought and brought to a triumphant conclusion the longest law suit in Ulster Civil law (originally started by our grandfather) against the monopoly of the fishing rights. The fishermen banded together and broke the London ring and now the lough is run as a co-operative, with each fisherman having a share and a licence. More men are eager to be fishermen now than live along the shore, but the occupation remains, as it always has (although for different reasons), within the desmesne of the men of the lough shore and their children. Before, fishing was a hereditary occupation and no one other than the families who lived alongside coveted it. Now it is a jealously guarded right, a gift within a new and, alas, greedy dispensation.

King has gone. But now there is a new danger; that of a barren lough. When we played there, around and along the very edge of the water there always glittered among the rushes a thin green spume of algae, a vivid growth that slid between your fingers before you could quite catch it. It is called glit, and this growth has now been overnourished to a monstrous lividly green richness by the cumulative effect of the fertilizers pouring into the water from the farmlands around.

Those children who play today along the lough shore can lift the glit in handfuls – it has lost that mercurial greenness that slipped so mysteriously between the fingers leaving only its emerald essence behind. Now it lies heavy and foreboding in the hand, and many of us fear that under its green pall the lough will soon stifle and die; but before that may happen, there is another horrid chance: so fiercely is the lough being fished that it is losing its balance and that soon there will be no eels, and that long line which reeled back to the Sargasso Sea and to Aristotle will finally be severed.

10

To the casual observer there is no ascent to the graveyard from the shore save by the little path that curves away around the hill, past the sloe-bushes up to the stile and back up to the Cross. But we know a secret route concealed by nettles, brambles and sloe-bushes that leads straight up, and we climb silently, one hand above the other, until we emerge from under the foliage, startling anyone who happens to be sitting on the raised tombstone near the path's secret exit and who only a moment before had seen us far below. It is a moment we relish. If, as so often happens, it is the Needle who is sitting there, he grumbles terribly. 'Bad cess to yous, up and down like the Creggan White Hare, you'd think yous had no place of your own to go home to.'

If the watchers on the tombstones are returned exiles, or people who have been displaced by the building of the aerodrome, but who come again and again to stare at the lough, they question us as to our breed, seed and generation and then consult and exclaim among themselves about our provenance and our resemblance to the older generation they remember. As they become engrossed in ancient genealogies we slip away and climb higher than any midges, to the very top of the crumbling stone walls of the old church which are so wide that they are more like small precipitous paths, covered in turf and daisies. There we lie for hours at a time hidden from reality, and from anyone below, spying, eavesdropping, dreaming and often it is true to say mourning, though God knows for what.

From the top of the wide ruined walls of the church and the graveyard where we lie for hours on long summer days, we can see the absolute boundaries of our world; on one side the flat reaches of the aerodrome stretching to the horizon, while if we look in the opposite direction we can see the far side of the lough, where the water and the sky melt at meeting, and only a series of faint blue lumps like bruises show where the spires and roofs of Lurgan touch the sky. So empty are the spaces between the horizons and so high the sky that its pale blue skin seems to bulge outwards. Behind it are those circles and beyond those the massy weight of Heaven, a Heaven which, according to our catechism (extremely nice on celestial geography) is jammed with angels and archangels, virtues and choirs, seraphim and cherubim piled atop each other in a rigid hierarchy of eternal worshippers, wings attached to their necks, their disembodied voices eternally chanting Hosannahs.

Just behind and below us skirting Ardboe Point is the New Road, white and glittering, driving straight towards the bulk of the pump house, and there joining up with the remnants of the Car 'Road, the old original way which meanders towards Golloman's Point. Car is the old word for any four-wheeled vehicle, and it must have been a bumpy enough ride along that rutted winding road, its deep ruts filled with gravel from the lough. Now its high spongey moss banks are dense with rushes, flowers and small wildlife, and willow and sally trees, and there is no traffic along it at all, since the New Road to the pump house has taken what little traffic there is. Half way along the Car Road widens into a small clearing, once the site of whitewashed thatched cottages full to overcrowding with large families. Now only three cottages are occupied; the others are ruined. The young men and women emigrated, the ones who were left went on living with their elders and parents, and grew old without getting married; and by the time their parents died they had imperceptibly become elders themselves, barren, rooted in routine, poverty and a bereft way of life in which chance, possibility and marriage had played no part.

The brilliant moss has almost covered the rounded stones laid like cobbles, and iris, daisies and bluebells grow right up to and over the ruined mounds. Old Sissy lives on her own in the first cottage. She is a widow and had ten children all of whom have emigrated to the United States and, like so many of the older generation, she often stands at her gate watching for whoever or whatever might come up or down the road. There is very little to watch for, now that the road is yielding back to nature. She is the last woman I ever see wearing the traditional peasant clothes of Northern Ireland; not the red flannel skirts and green silk petticoats favoured in fantastical lore about Ireland, but masses of shiny black stuff gathered into a long heavy skirt, a black blouse, and over the head and shoulders a big black fringed shawl. Once a woman donned those black garments she became a matriarch, ancient, sexless, biblical.

Each year Sissy's youngest daughter, Mary-Jane, who lives in New Jersey, comes home on a visit, and seeing them walking to Mass together – the venerable mother with white hair piled high in a circular nest, voluminous black bombazine skirts just clearing the ground, her home-made frame shoes giving her walk a characteristic step, and her daughter, in a new permanently pleated skirt, wedge-heeled shoes, pink short-sleeved blouse, her hair permed and mouth gleaming with Love That Pink – is to witness the gentle collision of two epochs.

Women like Sissy have their rituals. They are holy women, early to chapel, where they slip into the pews at the back, their heads bobbing under their shawls like a grounded rookery. Their rosary beads slip through their hands, their lips move through the ritual of the Rosary and its Mysteries and Hail Marys, but their eyes are roaming everywhere to see what conceits the younger ones are up to, and who is revealing what novelty, pretension or pregnancy. Even in our poverty-stricken district there are rigid distinctions in dress, and anyone who tries to bridge these gaps, or to ignore them, affords considerable amusement and derision, as well as calling forth a certain spite. Headscarves or shawls are the only acceptable headgear for women, except for the school-mistress who must wear a hat, or someone who considers herself a cut above the ordinary – a woman from another district perhaps, although such a visitor is rare. Any other young woman wearing a hat, or any other garment not considered suitable, is the subject of amusement and derision among the elders, and called a 'blade' or 'tackle'. The female elders form two distinct groups: the holy 'single' women who have never married and are great church-goers, and the married matriarchs. Both sects believe they have chosen the better part.

Children are not too observant about the fluctuating shapes of the grown-ups around them, but it was through Sissy's wasting away that I became aware of the body's mortality. Change is not a part of things for us, but one day walking down the Car Road, I suddenly perceived that Sissy, waiting as usual by her gate, had become a woman on a different scale, small and terribly mortal. 'We both suddenly noticed', Eiram says, 'it happened as quickly as that, and I remember you saying to her, "Sissy you've got so thin," and a look of pain crossed her face. She knew she was dying, that she'd got cancer, and she died within the year.'

At the end of the Car Road lies Golloman's Point, where my father owns another small farm. For us it is an enchanted place. In the small white house near the shore surrounded by elder-

101

bushes and sally trees lives Paddy Durrish, who possesses the cure or the charm – the inherited and arcane gift of healing certain ailments. Charms are magical attributes and powers passed from one member of a family to another; although if the person who possessed the cure was the last in the line, he or she could give it out to someone of his or her choice. It was an ambiguous gift, since, once you possessed it, you had to be available for whoever needed it, and there was no financial gain since the cure would disappear if paid for.

The custodian of the gift often possessed a seer's vision, knowing in advance what form of cure someone needed before they had made a formal request. Warts, painful backache, mysterious internal illnesses, 'chokings' and sicknesses in animals, could all be cured or treated, and as many people went to have such illnesses cured by a charm as went to a vet or the doctor – who after all lived many miles away and had to be paid.

My father is a sceptical man, and a truthful one. 'Two remarkable things happened in my experience with the cure', he said, 'and you must make of them what you will. Forty years ago Robert MacAllister and myself were driving the horses with the haylifter home from Matty's Hill. God knows how we manoeuvred that big lifter over those narrow keshes, but after we'd got over them I took a cussock of hay from the stack on the lifter behind me and chewed on it, and the seeds from it went down my throat, and got lodged there. I coughed all the way home, but it stayed stuck, and no matter how I wrought or drank, or coughed. I couldn't get the seeds or cussock neither up nor down. I coughed for three weeks till my mother said she couldn't stand listening to it any longer; she said why was I doing it, was it a new habit, or a bad cold or what? Robert too said "Why are you at that coughing, go you over to Durrish and get the cure."

'As soon as I walked in the door and before I spoke Durrish said, "Have you come about the cough?" I nodded. He got up and went into the other room; he stayed there only for about a minute. But in that minute I made a little cough, different from before, and I felt something come into my mouth. I spat it into my hand and there was the cussock and little knot of seeds I had been chewing three weeks before.

'Another time my bull got sick. Now that bull was worth a lot of money, well it was a fortune to me then – and was the only bull in this part of the country. One day without warning it fell down on its side panting, catching its breath, and a foam of bubbles appeared at the edges of its mouth. "Go you quick for the vet," I said to Robert. But he said, "If you wait till the vet gets here you won't have a bull, for it'll be dead long before that. Get you to Durrish." So I went straight over and again, as I ran in, before speaking he said: "You have come about your bull and it's choking. But it will be up and well when you get home." I went home, but was afraid to go up to the field where the bull was lying. Then I saw Robert running towards me across the field and I thought, it has died. But he was shouting "It's up, it's up, it's on its feet," and I found that it had stopped choking and catching its breath at the same time Durrish was talking to me.

'And yet again there was a man whose bull became ill – a man from outside the parish; and when he came to Durrish's door, Durrish met him and said, "No man can cure your bull. Go home at once, at once, and burn its carcass," and he went back, and it was dead with anthrax.'

Those cures and charms, so intrinsic and incorporeal a part of our life, have almost vanished, although we took them utterly for granted as a continuing noumenon. The reality of the power of the charm was based on a belief so old and profound that it came out of the time before St Colman rowed down the lough in search of solitude and a place remote from the world's distractions, and chose this lovely hill rising so sheer from the water, and mixed his mortar with the milk of a magic cow and built the Cross that pinned the parish on to the earth. But Durrish died years ago, and his son-in-law to whom he had passed the immemorial gift was blown up by a bomb in a pub, and the gift died with him.

Just before his house lies perhaps the most potent talisman of all – the stone of the hoof of the cow. Nearly every Sunday in spring and summer, all of us except our father, who never walks anywhere if he can help it, and certainly never for mere pleasure or exercise, go on an excursion to Golloman's Point to look at the stone.

The ritual is always the same. Ellen tries to collect us all together and make us look decent and clean for the walk with the mistress, and we congregate around the pram like starlings for what she calls a lick and promise. When we do finally set out we engage in an argument about who will push the vast and noisome pram containing the current baby and her filched belongings, although always after a few yards the victor loses interest and our mother takes over. We straggle around and behind squabbling and devising complicated games, sulking or joining in, forming and breaking new alliances until we reach the Cross and the parallel routes of the Car Road and the New Road. If it has been raining we walk along the New Road, since in wet weather the pram sinks to its axles in the Car Road, but we love the Car Road best, and meeting with Sissy and going into her little house with its white scrubbed settle and its farls of bread set to cool along the table. We go in to get a drink of water from the crock under the table, but our mother tries to discourage us from this since all Sissy's water has to be fetched from a well at the edge of the clearing. 'Let them drink, the cratures,' Sissy always says; and as we sip, we look at the room where she lives, so sparse, so clean, so warm.

Whichever road we choose we gather the fat triangular pods of the yellow flags that grow so thickly in the swampy soil and break them open to prise apart the seeds embedded within like clenched teeth. We meticulously pluck the mare's-tail plant into descending sections to make miniature Christmas trees or play talismanic rhyming and chanting games. Sometimes we bury specially marked or unusually shaped pieces of wood in niches and crevices under the water to induce them to petrify, keeping a wary eye out for the swans who nest all along the edge and who, we believe, constantly lust after a chance to break arms with their wings. There is a legend that the lough water petrifies wood, that after seven years it hardens into stone. Each Sunday we hide our wood and mark the spot carefully so that we will find it metamorphosed. It is still there for all I know. Seven years then was always too far in the future; now, it is too far back.

To reach Golloman's Point we climb up an incline, a remarkable enough feature in our level unflurried landscape where only Ardboe Point is prominent. But even more extraordinary is that this little slope is cleft by a deep and narrow chasm, called

104

Carswiggy, almost concealed by the overgrowth of ivy, elder, briony and whin-bushes which grow up to and down its sides and meet across its divide. We always hope that something or someone unwary will be found splattered at the bottom, and one memorable day what we have covertly longed for happens. One of my father's cows falls into Carswiggy gap. The cows are the most valuable assets on all the farms around, precious and valuable animals, and my father is proud of his. When he hears that one of his best heifers has fallen into Carswiggy, he is frantic. As the news spreads, the fishermen come running up from the lough shore and from neighbouring cottages, to clamber up and down the gully with hectic hands and faces; their shouting and cursing mingle with my father's lamentations and the painful lowing of the beast from the green depths below. We watch with appalled and tender interest as the dead cow is raised, its small udder flopping, its open milky eyes glazed, its legs dangling like broken sticks, and grieve that we have missed the actual crash of the beast into the ravine.

'She wasn't a high cow then, she was very low indeed,' a sister observes, pretending to be sage; and from then on, whenever we are called upon to explain the meaning of Ardboe the definition takes on a second layer of meaning and association, and guilty mirth. The first meaning has to do with magic. Just before the road ends at Golloman's Point, half-hidden in the grass lies the Stone, the great climactic point of our walk – a magic bequest from the past. Deeply and clearly embedded in it is the imprint of a cow's hoof.

We know the story backwards, but need to have it retold every Sunday. The magic cow, the High Cow of Ardboe, much coveted by others who are jealous of its powers and of the posterity it will bestow on its monastic owners, is stolen away in the dead of night. As the thieves lead her away she miraculously leaves the imprint of her hooves on the stones in her path so that when her loss is discovered the pursuing monks can follow her twisting lough-shore route. They rescue her and bring her back and the revered stone, the last fragment of that miraculous trail, has lain there, it is said, and we believe it, for over a thousand years.

We are always gratifyingly moved by the story, by its antiquity, its satisfactory conclusion, its assertion of right over wrong, and the moral implications contained in that eerie cloven print set so clearly into the stone. Looking at it, it seems as though the lough's legendary petrifying qualities were so potent then that even pliable clay could have been transmogrified into permanence. I went back to search for the stone recently, to resurrect this magic relic, but it had gone. I felt no surprise at that disappearance. No stolen cow would cleave the rock today.

With Sissy's death the house on the Car Road seemed suddenly to crumble: only the two old brothers Ned and John Curran, who was famous as a rhymester and spoke naturally in rhyming couplets, and Forbie, an old man without kin, were left living there in adjoining houses that began to drift downwards surrounded by silence. One day on the way home from school we met John Curran, dazed, grimy, weeping.

'Two great men are lately dead, Father Walsh and our Ned,' he said sorrowfully, and we laughed at his poetic habit not knowing he was speaking the truth and that the parish priest and his brother had died at exactly the same time. He was dead himself within a month. Only old Forbie was left in his house, and one day came to my parents in distress. His straw and rush thatched roof had begun to drift to the ground and the rain was coming in. My parents went back with him and found that his blue and white willow pattern plates, his only treasure, had been shattered by two adolescent boys who had wandered aimlessly up the Car Road and, seeing the open door, the collapsed roof, taken the place for empty. He came to live with us, in a little cottage at the end of our rampar; and he too contributed to our mythology about cows and their sacredness.

The far side of the lough was a most mysterious place to us – although we knew that in earlier days, before King had wielded such power, the fishermen had fished both sides of the lough. During the season when there was no fishing, when the fish were spawning or the eels were hibernating, times were hard indeed. To earn a few shillings the fishermen would dig gravel from the lough, pan it out into the bottom of their boats and so laden, dangerously heavy, would row over to Lord Pakenham's estate at Langford Lodge on the opposite shore hoping that the overseer there would buy their gravel; which he frequently did. One day, a small mischief was done on the estate and the fishermen who had delivered a load of gravel, one of whom was Forbie, were blamed and told to return no more.

Although the poor money they earned by hauling the gravel was wholly disproportionate to the labour involved, there was no other way to earn any. Forbie and his mate Packy were desperate and on the next fine day set off with their gravel hoping to appease the foreman at Langford. As they rowed up the narrow inlet they saw a cow grazing near the shore. Forbie and Packy anchored, jumped on to land and dragged the beast into the water; Forbie held her there while Packy ran up to the estate to warn the workers that a cow was drowning. As the hue and cry approached, Forbie began to save the cow – and for their efforts he and Packy were given tea in the kitchen, their gravel was bought, and the ban was lifted.

I used to lie on the top of the gravestones gazing out at the far side of the lough where such things had happened, and dreamed of going there. When I got there I discovered that the far side of the lough must always be far away, on the other side from wherever you are.

By the time our weekly walks ended the cottages were almost overgrown with moss and memories. They had been built from mud and mortar and whitewashed with lime, and their roofs were made of a rushy thatch woven tight and neat and waterproof. So long as they were lived in, these cottages were snug and warm. But once they were abandoned, after a very short time the damp attacked the roofs and the houses slithered gently back into the earth, leaving at last only their own memorials in the shape of mounds covered by a matted and vivid moss, which seemed to pull them back from the last jealous strain of the earth.

11

We often call in at the graveyard on the way back from Eglish to say a prayer at the family grave, to examine the Pin Tree, and afterwards to walk sedately behind our mother pushing the pram to where she likes to sit for a while on a certain tombstone that lies like a broad shelf against the outside walls of the ruined church, and which has been polished by centuries of such use. The bulk of the church walls protect anyone sitting there from winds from all quarters, and on most Sundays another person has usually already found haven there before we arrive. This tombstone is on the highest point around the lough shore, and we have noticed, since we were old enough to notice, that once an adult sits down here and gazes out over the vistas below and before, he or she becomes quieter and more at rest, as though in church.

Immediately below, many precipitate feet below, are the sally-trees, and the inlets with their boats lying still, and further away the reaches of Golloman's Point, with its houses hidden among the tall bushes that grow almost to the shoreline; beyond that is the Washing Bay and then the smudged bulk of the flat lands around Maghery and Coalisland. There are no boats on the lough – the fishermen rarely go out on Sunday unless the weather has been so bad as to preclude the lifting of their lines for days before, and no one goes sailing for pleasure. Even the concept is impossible.

The presence of another person sitting on the gravestone is a further sign of the apartness of Sunday. The graveyard is no longer our private domain. It becomes a much more public place, and its holiness, of which we are always somewhat conscious, becomes its pre-eminent condition. All day a slow sift of people come to pay their respects to their dead, to lay flowers on their graves, to kneel in remembrance, and to say a practical prayer for those of their family who lie below, and those, far more numerous, who have died far away.

The words 'death' and 'dead' are not much used in the parish.

The descriptive phrases used instead are not euphemisms to disguise a horrid truth, but are descriptions of the state the dead are now in; words like 'deceased', 'departed this life', and 'resting in peace' have real meaning when life is viewed as a stopping-place. All deaths in the parish are announced from the altar as passionately personal losses. 'Dearly beloved brethren,' the priest says, 'your prayers are requested for the soul of our late dearly beloved sister [or brother] who delivered her soul to God on Thursday.' Everyone kneels and prays that he or she may rest in peace. These prayers for the dead, whether in church or by a graveside, are not murmurings of remembrance. They are said for practical purposes – to help the dead reach the place their souls are seeking. We are taught that every prayer said specifically for a dead soul does specifically help that soul, by decreasing the fierceness of the shriving flame of Purgatory already consuming the black shadow of sin in order that it can fuse with the brightness of God. Such power to reach across the gulf of the grave and deliver comfort is also presumably a powerful alleviation for the pain and grief of those left behind.

Near to the entrance of the graveyard stands the Pin Tree, already at the time of which I write beginning to wither and die from a combination of extreme old age, tender abuse and oxide poisoning. Every inch of its bark from root level to high above our heads is studded with pins, nails, medals, money and any small flat objects that can be hammered into it. Small incisions made so that farthings and sixpences could be pushed in have, with the tree's growth, expanded and healed into clefts like fat pursed lips, with only the tiny gleam of the bevelled edge of the coin to be seen in their depths. Where a hole has been cut out of the bark so that a coin could be inserted flat under it the skin of the bark has repaired itself all around, like the cuticle round a nail; parts of the tree look like a living housing for a series of round copper miniatures. Between these incisions and insertions, and the studded chain-mail of nails and rivets, countless initials and dates have been carved and whittled and these too have swollen and split as the tree grew.

We know every inch of the tree and can spot a new addition from a distance. Sometimes someone leaves a florin – a two-shilling piece – presumably to buy bigger and better luck, which it does in a way, for those among us who are liberated enough from superstition or the effects of magic as to be able to lever out the coins to buy more tangible goods. None of us sisters could or would have done it; scrupulousness, cowardice, the knowledge that these coins were the repositories for hopes and wishes, prevented us; we did not want to steal a burden of dreams, and we never put a coin or a pin in the tree, nor put our names on it. But, even if we had not had such metaphysical deterrents, the coins were so bent and scratched from being hammered into the tree that if they were levered out their appearance would have proclaimed their misbegotten provenance.

The tree is supposed by some to have water-power – that is, that the water lying in its hollows possesses the curative petrifying powers of lough water – as well as wishing-power, and few people leave the graveyard without depositing their talisman.

There are no graves near the Pin Tree; perhaps its pagan magic radiates a certain distance into the Christian territory surrounding it or, as seems more likely, the older beliefs that survive in this high place have been pushed back into this circle; the containment has maybe made it more potent. Just outside the circle cast by the shadow of its leaves (a shadow that gets smaller and less dense each year of our childhood) lie the little tumuli of kinfolk, and scattered among them the new gravestones, and newest of all the shiny inscribed memorial monuments.

We know every burial place in the graveyard and the nuances and niceties implicit in the positions and placings of the markers above them. The oldest graves of all are the tumuli, some of which are marked at their limits by stones brought up from the lough shore, with faint daubs of whitewash apparent in their folds; then there are horizontal stone and slate slabs, some lying flat on the ground, some on stone supports which in many cases have collapsed, leaving the slabs tilted. When we are not lying on top of the church walls, we lie on these crazy graven beds, idly hoking the moss out of ancient incisions, deciphering names as familiar as our own through their living descendants.

The higher the slabs are from the ground the newer they are; and newest of all are those which stand upright with gold lettering;

these more elaborate memorials are a signal of a family's material advancement in the world. Some of these graves have been made even more alien by a plethora of wax flowers under glass domes. These newer graves (or rather, graves that have had money spent on them, for there are no new graves, all the plots having been bespoke for generations) are rigid in their outline, with ledges of polished slate and granite surrounding an inlay of white pebble and glittery mica; whereas the older graves look as though the bodies below them have been peacefully absorbed. Staring at the bleak and ersatz grandeur of the revamped graves, we feel that the corpses beneath them must lie uncomforted within their unyielding outlines, and we resolve never to allow anything but soil and grass to cover us.

The graves go right up to the old ruined walls of the church and continue inside, and as over the centuries the soil has been dug and dug again and more bodies have been interred, so the level of the earth has crept halfway up the walls. The windows which once were high above the assembled monks are now at waist level, festooned with garlands of ivy, periwinkle and bindweed. There is no doubt in our minds that this is the best, the only place to be buried in, here among these faded, half-buried and tilted advertisements for the dead, in this lovely encroachment on to ground even more sanctified than that outside the walls.

The church floor is a living *millefleurs* tapestry. Some of the graves are smooth and turf-covered, others are shaggy with wild grasses, and between them grow white and purple clover, sweet cicely – the stems of which we crush to inhale the smell of aniseed – and sorrel, which although we eat in quantities from hedgerows we never touch inside the graveyard. There are daisies too and periwinkle and speedwell and multitudes of dandelion and nipplewort and wild raspberry bushes and hypericum.

I wish with all my heart that our family plot was inside the church, but it is just inside the graveyard gate, near the old Cross. Beside it is the grandest of all graves and the most terrible and bleak. This is the Treanors' tomb, a marble platform reached by a shallow flight of steps with a copy of a Celtic cross surrounded by railings on top. It is falling to pieces, but it still has a shocking decayed grandeur not unlike that possessed by Lizzie, the last of the Treanors, who defied the steam-rollers and any other form of authority.

Our plot is surrounded by a rambling privet hedge and is overgrown and sadly neglected. Every time she passes it, our mother bewails its state and chivvies our father and us to tidy it, but the only time we do is just before the annual open-air Mass followed by Benediction held in front of the old church, attended by nearly everyone from both ends of the parish. The only other times that the whole parish is united is at the Lammas Fair held in August outside the gates of our house, and at midnight Mass at Christmas held in the parish church in Upper Ardboe.

The rare gathering of the people of the upper and lower parishes shows very clearly that even within the containedness of Ardboe there are two distinct races – the black-haired Celts who came from the sea down the river Bann, and the fairer-skinned, fairer-haired people who had come up the Bann from the South of Ireland. The fair-haired people often have the name Bann – Gaelic for white – tacked on to their Christian name, and the darker families are called the Dubhs, meaning black.

There are two kinds of nicknames in the district – those ancient Gaelic ones which identify clans by their recurring physical characteristics, and the later English ones, which are often witty, always apt and sometimes cruel. These are never used to the bearer's face, and there is a scrupulous convention observed that no one is aware of his own nickname. Toodles and the Rung, the Cord and the Tallyman, the Old Horse, Riley, Lloddelley, the Painter, the Lurk, all these are useful as well as being descriptive. In a parish where many families bear the same surnames, and where Christian names are limited to those of saints with a special place in Irish devotions – Patrick, Bridget, Mary, Colum, Thomas, Kieran, Peter, Teresa – they are also necessary. If a stranger enquires for a man by his official family name, people are often hard put to place him. In any case, everyone – except the Needle in his voluble role as keeper of the Cross – is reticent with strangers and their enquiries, and we all know to keep a look-out for officials from the Broo, the unemployment bureau, who sometimes drive into our lower reaches to see if anyone receiving unemployment benefit is working. They leave bemused a short while later.

The nickname we are most fascinated by is borne by a man whom we have never met – Sleekit, who becomes a glossily urbane apocryphal figure in our lives. '*Why* Sleekit?' we ask. 'Robin because he has red hair, and the Cork because he's light; but Sleekit?'

'Because his skin shone, his hair was always like patent leather and he *was* sleek,' my father would say. 'He also had twenty-two children,' he added thoughtfully. Sleekit seems such an odd word, not common coinage in our word currencies, and not applicable to anyone we knew, who on the whole were like us, shaggy.

Gaelic words run all through our language, an old faded strand among the English tongue. The use of Gaelic in the countryside both in these nicknames and in the naming of townlands (Killy-colpy, the woody hill; Mullinahoe, the hill of the little cave; Killmascally, wood of the shadows; Lurgyroe, townland of the red-haired people; Killy-canavan, the wild wood; Bornamona, the bog road) all testify as much to poverty and the remoteness of the parish as to the ethnological origins of its inhabitants.

Ardboe was too poor and too wild to have been lived in by the Scottish Presbyterian and English immigrants who took over the land but lived in prettier places. Whenever we pass on the way to Cookstown a largish house surrounded by garden, trees and fertile fields which, we believe, once belonged to our family before we had to yield it because of our allegiance to the Faith, I look at it with malice and wish its occupants ill. I remember wondering bitterly, when I read Edmund Curtis's observation in his *History of Ireland* that 'the Irish are the longest settled on their own soil of any race in Europe', how the word 'settled' could be used for a race that in their own country became the dispossessed. I conveniently forget, as I savour my resentment, that we bear the name of the place where we live and have always lived.

The celebratory annual ritual of the abbey Mass and Benediction is high theatre. Earlier in the day the fishermen have set up a trestle table along one wall of the old church and erected all

113

around it an arch and trellis made of branches and ivy. The more devout women of the parish, two of whom, Philomena and Matty, are the sacristans of the church, have festooned this arch with garlands of ivy, leaves and flowers, and laid white lace tablecloths held down by white stones over the surface of the table, and scattered it, too, with flowers. It looks more like a pagan shrine in which to celebrate the rollicking excesses of Pan and Bacchus than an altar for the modest ritual that we will attend rather than participate in; for in these pre-Vatican II days, the Mass is celebrated with the celebrant's back turned towards the congregation, excluding us from witnessing the mysterious Sacrament taking place. Benediction is a more glorious affair with priests and altar boys facing the people. Towards the end of the afternoon, as though they have suddenly become aware of the profane or pagan aspect of the altar, the women make a floral embroidery along the front of the altar cloth: 'Jesus have Mercy' is written in ivy, periwinkle, daisies and briony.

All evening our straggling road has been filled with the congregation making its early way to the graveyard to get a good vantage point or a flat tombstone to sit on during the sermon – which no one will hear, since the wind that blows in from the lough, mild though it is, whips away the words as they leave the priest's mouth. The dogs that normally lie so undisturbed in the middle of the road are crouched along the side, and the Dally's dog barks forlornly from where he has been shut in for the duration.

We are extremely ambivalent about the whole event. We love the importance that is conferred on the place by the Mass and the gathering of the parish, but we are consumed with jealousy about the invasion of the graveyard and are at a loss to know how to assert out mastery of this turf. We are burning to be acknowledged as the proper inhabitants and possessors of the place. But no one takes a blind bit of notice of our posturing endeavours except other children, who swagger where they will, thoroughly defeating our purpose.

As the afternoon draws on the atmosphere becomes increasingly tense and anticipatory; and just before the ceremony begins the altar boys in black cassocks and white surplices put the Bible and the chalice, the ciborium and the temporary tabernacle in place of the stones on the altar. In their fluttering white lace they move with supreme self-consciousness and seem so utterly removed from the boys we know and play with in the school-yard that they could be newly arrived from a strange land. I resent their importance, their inclusion in the scheme of importance. I hope they will trip and fall with the ciborium or chalice, although I dread the cataclysm when the Host hits the ground and all Heaven breaks loose.

The priests robe themselves inside the ruined walls and then follow their acolytes out, swinging censers with abandon, so that the fumes of incense envelop us and the subtle and extraordinary noise of open-air prayer begins. The intonations, the declamatory Latin, the murmured responses, the stirrings and rustlings and coughing so pronounced inside the chapel at ordinary Mass, but here drifting quietly upwards to join the cawings of the rooks and seagulls, the hum of the incense-scented midges, all combine to make a far more intoxicating and mystical mingling of atmosphere and noise than any cathedral ceremony. There is something exquisite about the occasion – the antiquity of the site, the apparent simplicity of the ceremony, the devout attentiveness of the congregation. Their interrelatedness and tribal bonds make it like a marriage, a contract between God and man or the reiteration of a treaty between earth and sky and water and people.

When it is over the congregation is reluctant to leave, to step back into the separate ordinariness of life. And the separations start as soon as they go out through the graveyard gate and the women begin the return home with their children; those men who are not drinkers follow the women in clusters. Many of these men are members of an organization called the Pioneers founded by a priest in the nineteenth century to try to combat the dreadful problem of alcoholism in Ireland. Members renounced alcohol in all forms for life, and those who attended the monthly meetings were on the whole young men who had already recognized that a problem existed, and wished to avoid it; they wished to better themselves, and had thus already arrived at a measure of self-respect. Members wore the Pioneer badge, a little white enamel plaque with a burning heart – the symbol of the passion of Jesus – in their lapel. They continued their journey up the road – but many of the other men gathered in the back room of the pub for the business of drink, and there they remained for the rest of the evening.

It was – and is – against the law to drink in public houses on Sunday. Indeed all the licensing laws in Northern Ireland seemed deliberately designed to preempt or curtail comfort and relaxation in the only public meeting-places available then to most people. The laws reflected the nature of the men who passed them – the dour Protestant ministers of the governing party – but reflected too the need for repressive legislation to prevent any gathering of men after dark. Such meetings have for so long in Ireland been the breeding-ground and drilling-ground for clandestine and rebellious movements and for secret societies. Pubs by law had to close by nine o'clock, which meant that on summer nights the fishermen had not finished setting their lines, and in winter they only just reached the pub by bicycle before it was time to leave again. Deep in the countryside, far from police patrols, the licensing laws were ignored and most country pubs closed at midnight or after. Occasionally a lone policeman came cycling out on a desultory visit from the barracks in Coagh, a village five miles away, but word of his coming preceded him and by the time he cycled past the men were sitting on the grassy banks on each side of the road with their glasses in their hands viewing his slow progress up Biddy's Brae with amiable solicitude. They watched him cycle as far as the Cross, turn around and cycle back, and as soon as he had turned the corner at the Cross Roads they streamed back into the pub to continue their crack. Sometimes two policemen came cycling leisurely along just before closing-time, and then they were bought as much drink as they could manage – and, if at all possible, more.

There was always a great deal of singing, and in the evening when we brought out a mug of tea from the house to the pub, a hundred yards away, we would hear old men singing songs or reciting verses. We knew them all, the singers and the songs, but we thought of them as the embarrassing outbursts of men stocious with drink. Only when we grew up and left home and looked back were we able to appreciate, at an irrecoverable remove, the secret life that subsisted in that deep countryside – the music of

116

a hidden Ireland with its complex harmonies and quavering grace-notes, the passionate concealed underground life of another country whose difference was deceptive, because the common language seemed the same.

If the men in the pub were asked to sing these songs when they were sober they would become what they called 'bashful'. 'They're only auld come-all-yees', they'd say, 'rubbidgy old songs. Yous don't want to hear them.' Such attitudes obtained all over Ireland. When music producers from Radio Eireann, the Irish radio station, went around the country in the 1950s in the vanguard of the folk-boom to record the fiddlers, the tin whistlers, the pipers, the singers of the countryside, they found an enormous reservoir of talent. But the people were often reluctant to reveal themselves as traditional musicians, because such music was despised; and some fiddle-players went to join fellow musicians with their fiddles hidden under their coats because they were ashamed to be seen.

The ritual preceding and during these outbursts of songs in the pub was always the same. A fisherman, his natural bashfulness dissipated by the Guinness in his veins, would suddenly be moved to sing and would rise shakily to his feet. Gradually the talk would die down and, swaying slightly, eyes closed, and often supported by a nearby but equally unstable friend, he would embark on the ceremonial song. The manner of singing and the reception of the song were governed by convention, ritual and ceremony. Men caught in mid-sentence by the giving voice would stop, tilt their heads, and remain frozen from the sounding of the first notes till the end, which was often an unconscionably long time coming. The songs were plaintive, slow, lamenting, and during the long pauses there were certain acceptable phrases of encouragement launched towards the singer: 'Good man yerself,' or 'You're a brev man,' or sometimes a reiteration of the last words of the verse, all of which served as a kind of chorus, necessary for the esteem of the singer and the continuation of his song. At its end a swell of voices would repeat the same phrases, the highest praise being 'By God and he *can* sing,' although there were occasionally murmurs of dissent especially if someone used this precious phrase about someone who actually could not sing, but was so drunk as to forget this fact. Even then the listeners, though bored and amused by the singer's conceit, observed the formalities and politenesses, although occasionally a recalcitrant voice might mutter, 'He's none at all.'

Eiram and Barry Paul always knew more folk-songs than the rest of us, and could sing them so beautifully that they were frequently sent for to sing in the pub. Later Barry became one of the best known folk-rock musicians in Ireland; but Eiram looking back said:

'I feel a real sense of loss about what *we* missed out on when we were growing up because of our peculiar position in the community. When I went back later with friends, deliberately in search of that secret life, and heard marvellous exponents like Arthur Ryan playing the fiddle, when I went to the ceilidhs that had always taken place but which we had never been to, I realized what I'd always known, but had never discovered – that a secret other life has been going on all the time, which we missed partly because it wasn't regarded, partly because we were cut off from it by our expectations, our education, our position as children of our parents. This secret hidden life, that still exists in Ireland, is exceedingly important to the continuing life of Ireland – the thing that makes Ireland Irish.'

A pub still stands on the same site. The old one was burnt down with its great copper-banded barrels and old trade-marked mirrors and, for us worst loss of all, the loft above with its store of secret books, elaborate photograph albums, volumes of *Household Etiquette*, early magazines and old newspapers; Victorian stories for children, copies of Ripley's *Believe it or Not*, all jettisoned from the main house over the years. Up there in that dusty room under the eaves, with its discarded furniture, its old mattresses on which the strange stray dogs and cats as well as the accredited many who have attached themselves to the household lay sleeping in warm peace, occasionally scratching at fleas which jumped on to our legs to Ellen's dismay, we too lay sucking in irrelevant information as though it were oxygen. Some of the things we read there gave us nightmares, but we found little that had anything to do with the movements and yearnings of our minds towards a real world outside. Below us we could hear the cough of the men in the bar room, the clash of glass on the counter, the murmur of conversations, but up there we were locked into a strange phantasmagorical contending world of our own.

The new pub, built in the old one's place and which does not belong to my father, is as hideous as any other new small building in Ireland. No policeman would cycle leisurely down that road now, and it is many years since there was an officer of the Royal Ulster Constabulary in the pub. Ardboe is a Republican area. Only convoys of trucks full of soldiers with rifles at the ready come down that road now with helicopters hovering above, and when they go into the pub to do a search they are covered by soldiers kneeling on those same grassy banks where men who have since been blown to pieces by a bomb once knelt, and where Wee Harry boasted about shooting the local banshee and ducked his head and smiled, placating, as the Law rode slowly by.

12

In many houses along the road that leads from the Cross to the chapel and school there is at least one person who is 'odd' or astray. Sometimes whole families, inbred for generations, lead strange existences unconnected with reality. 'There is no harm in them,' is what is always said of these old or prematurely old men and women, wistful and sad, who have long since abandoned or forfeited thoughts of marriage and children. Their upbringing and conditioning, the constraints of religion, the lack of a feasible future, seem profoundly to have damaged the courage and sense of self necessary to contemplate such a step; many have eked out their lives without ever having had a romantic or sexual relationship with another person. It's an old story in our old district and all over Ireland. The average age at which couples got married in Ireland remained remarkably higher than anywhere else in Europe for over a century (until the mid-1960s), and the number of men who died unmarried was significantly higher.

The three old brothers, cousins of our grandfather, who live in a little house along the Car Road are the living reality of such statistics. They are all shy – Tom, the youngest, pathologically so – and their wrinkled, weather-beaten, shuttered faces under ancient flat checked caps have a diffident inconsequence, as though it would be too presumptuous of them to allow the experience and the pain of their lives to affect their faces and expression. Pain there is, if only in the lost negotiations buried in their own and their country's past. Their only luxury appears to be cigarette-smoking. Even this dubious pleasure of the senses is a silent and shadowy affair, since they are afraid to smoke indoors lest they should be seen by a stranger and so they go into the fields behind the house in order to 'light up', as smoking is always called. This departure from any company in the house is unacknowledged; they slip out like wraiths. Even on the coldest of days and evenings we can see the tiny spirals of smoke rising from the fields beyond their house, but we never see the smokers.

One night on the way to Evening Devotions I hear Tom speak, and it is the first and last time I ever hear his voice. Devotions are a church service held every night of the week during October, and nearly everyone goes to them, save whatever member of each family has to stay behind to look after the house and children too young to attend. All along the stretch of road so familiar by day and so often deserted we can see the black outline of couples or groups of people bulking against the surface of the road and the low horizon, both silvered by moonlight. There is an occasional murmur of conversation, a burst of laughter, but otherwise all is silence. Sometimes a man or woman on a bicycle goes noiselessly by, giving us a turn, since few bikes have lights and it is not till they are almost on top of you that you hear the sibilant turn of the wheels on the tarmac.

The church is a mile and a half away and we run exhilarated through the starry darkness, our behaviour devoid of the restraints and normalities of daylight. We look up at the Milky Way, and search for shooting stars and the outlines of the fairy trees. We know that a shooting star means there has been a displacement in

120

the firmament, and that through the small gap left by the star's tumble a soul, its yearning finally finished, can make and mark its narrow escape to God. I think of the fearful unrestrained soul exploding upwards, wonder from what part of the world it has made its ascent and cross myself. The act is a release from hopeful melancholy and introspection, and I join my sisters and the Dallys and the Corrans and the MacAllisters; we hide in the ditches and hedgerows and gaps, or crouch behind gates and tremble lest we not be found. We run away from each other and hold our breath, and whisper stories of Black Dogs and the Living Dead that friends of friends have met, and of the Devil's appearance, and the Banshee's cry, and we hold hands as we pass the fairy trees at the Moor Hill and move closer to the nearest group of adults in a black clump ahead of us.

From the top of the Moor Hill (which is no more than the merest incline) the low meadows stretch to Eddie Ban's farm opposite. The eldest of Eddie Ban's daughters – there are no sons – has just married a young, energetic and ambitious farmer from Upper Ardboe whose farming methods, although hardly radical, seem in their progressiveness alien and threatening. They shake the air around his farm, and this feeling of incipient disturbance is justified later when he buys a tractor and begins to tear up old hedges and level off old hillocks and drain ancient marshes; if he did not his farm would not survive economically, but no one can forgive him – not for the disturbance to the landscape but because he makes a success out of the old farm.

His latest innovations are big new barns and byres lit by strong pressure lamps with the brand-name of Tilley. Shy Tom, who helps with the milking, lights them each night. They are a great technological advance, for there is no electricity in the district and oil-lamps and lanterns are used everywhere; in the darkness (which had a black intensity, since vanished from the countryside with the advent of electricity) the new lights blare like a triumphant cry.

The Dally brothers are walking silently ahead of us and as we run past we hear Joseph say: 'Therem's quare big new lights over by the Eddie Ban's, I wonder what name bees on them.' The fairy tree is passed. We look away and wait, breath bated, for surely

121

Tom must speak. But there is only silence. Then, just as we reach the chapel graveyard Tom clears his throat. 'Tilley,' he says, 'Tilley'; we rùn into the church triumphant.

Just up the road in the other direction lives another old cousin, called Gulliver because he wanders both in mind and body, especially at the time of the full moon when he becomes moon-mad. We are wary of him, for although he is a gentle creature his movements and actions are startling and unpredictable. Sometimes an inarticulate noise will break from his throat, an alarming cascade of noise, or he will suddenly begin to run, as though he has espied something he is searching for; but as quickly he stops, a look of desolation on his face, his oasis gone. His body is permanently twisted by some birth or genetic defect, his head tilted strangely on his neck, his face pulled into prismatic planes and angles, and we do not wonder that his thoughts are crazy in such a container.

There are other old people who are so shy – or modest, as the affliction is called – that they keep their heads down when they meet us, as though they will become invisible; one old woman makes strange involuntary noises at arbitrary intervals, particularly noticeable during Mass and especially at the climax of the silent Consecration. She is reputed to have swallowed a penny, which has remained stuck in her gullet, and the strange guttural noises erupting through the chapel are served as a warning on us not to go sucking pennies. All of these, numerous as they are, are a tiny proportion compared to the others who try to find some consolation in alcohol for the wastage of their lives, the dwindling of hope and ambition. Although our community accepts and accommodates manifestations of madness without question, it cannot easily accept any voluntary deviations from its narrow conventions and moral codes. Anyone who through high spirits, talent, frustrations, ambition, a desire to shock or an indestructible sense of style breaches the behaviour barriers becomes the target of biting scorn and ire: he or she has no 'modesty' or is an 'amadan' or a 'kitterdy'.

At school one of the first poems we learned was W. B. Yeats's 'Lake Isle of Innisfree', the expression of the poet's yearning for a return to a lost world that never existed, a paradise filled with the low hum of bees about their propagating business. What brought on this attack of memory, Miss Rogers told us, was Yeats hearing some water trickling down a shop-window as he walked down the Strand. In London, years later, I opened a book in a shop in the Strand and read that since the beginning of this century there have been twice as many people in mental hospitals in the Irish Republic as in England and Wales, proportionate to the populations. Among eight different immigrant minorities studied in Canada, schizophrenia was always more common in Catholic than in Protestant females. The researcher who revealed these statistics suggested that perhaps Catholic teaching may be at odds with the wider cultural beliefs and demands of society. Oliver Gillie, the author of *Who Do You Think You Are?*, wrote:

The high frequency of schizophrenia among the Irish Catholics in Canada cannot be explained away as a result of the stress of immigration itself, since the Irish at home also have a greater than normal tendency to become schizophrenic. A genetic predisposition to schizophrenia also seems unlikely: the Irish tend to develop schizophrenia before the normal age of marriage, which is late in Ireland. The chances of people marrying and having children are lower once they have had a period of mental illness, so the chances of their genes being passed on to the next generation are also lower. Therefore a genetic predisposition could not account for the high frequency of schizophrenics in Ireland . . . it is only possible to speculate on the cause of the tendency for Irish Catholics to become schizophrenic. Catholicism itself may be an important cause.

As I read, there rose before my eyes my lake isle with its wounded modest people for whom peace never came dropping at all and only pain lay at the deep heart's core.

The doctors and researchers who still speculate whether Catholicism is directly connected to the extraordinary prevalence of schizophrenia and mental illness in Ireland have surely not been reared in the ways and practices of Irish Catholicism that obtained until recently, in which everything was coiled in on itself, and religion, history and social conditions were entwined in a mesh that entangled one further the more one struggled to get free. The Catholic faith in Ireland, although it has fanatical adherence to Rome and the Pope as its visible head on earth, is a religion on its own. Its history of social ostracism, the legal persecution that

123

drove it underground where it had to nourish itself on itself, has nurtured it into something more obsessive than the Catholic faiths of other countries that have continued to grow in the light.

Reading Tocqueville's *Letters from Ireland* many years after I had ceased to breathe that old unchronological air I came across a sentence spoken by a priest to Tocqueville in 1832. 'The Protestants hold that we love the dark; they will soon see that we do not fear the light.' But over a hundred years later we still lived in the dark. Geographical isolation, persecution, the extraordinary courage and tenacity of its practitioners, the prevalence of terror, the threat of punishment gave Catholicism a profound sentimental and patriotic appeal. For the decades when the Penal Laws were in force it was, after all, the only thing that Irish Catholics could call their own, although to do so was to risk persecution. And when with the passage of time and the swing of events it became the established religion of Ireland it retained elements of fanaticism as part of its creed – an absolute belief in its own rightness, a refusal to compromise or to see another person's point of view, a belief that anyone outside its tenets was an enemy or a betrayer. It also acquired a woeful capacity for dispensing not grace (although it professed to do that), but guilt.

Jesus, the King-pin of our religion, was fed into our imagination from the earliest age as a victim rather than a teacher. 'But a glorious victim, girls' – Father Lappin is exultant – 'a glorious victim, and it is his triumph that he has been assailed in a most brutal manner.' That bloody assault, his slow death on the Cross, is ceaselessly described with pious and loving relish, its gruesome details lingered over, not that we may appreciate love, but that we may apprehend the full extent of our sins and the enormity of the sacrifice needed to redeem them. Each one of us has inflicted a lash, driven in a thorn, a nail. The words seem to tumble from the priest's throat as he builds up the word-pictures for our delectation and to stir us to remorse.

There is visual evidence in plenty too – at school and in chapel we are surrounded by religious pornography, explicit images, lavish, potent and sexual, showing in sadistic detail the progress of the Passion of Our Lord. Spears enter flesh, thorns pierce the bowed head, muscular soldiers whip the acquiescent red-robed

124

man who forever stumbles under the weight of an enormous cross. Almost all the statues in church depict saints holding open garments to reveal a bleeding heart, benignly clasping the instrument of their torture with peerless resignation. And these images have more power and impact in our lives than they could ever have in other cultures where there is a tradition of visual images and paintings and decoration. There is no such tradition in our part of Ireland: how things look is of little account. The only coloured pictures on most people's walls are a picture of Our Lady of Perpetual Succour, a grisly picture of Jesus as a doe-eyed, long-haired man with his heart exposed and surrounded by flame, and a romantic impression of the men of the 1916 Rising defending the General Post Office in Dublin, which is regarded in much the same religious light as the other two.

Perhaps the most vivid of all our religious icons are the fourteen Stations of the Cross, three-dimensional panels hanging at intervals around the inside walls of the church and depicting the crucial episodes in Christ's journey from Golgotha to Calvary. To 'do the Stations' is to follow the symbolic path of the Passion, and is both a way of gaining indulgences and a vivid and moving aid to contemplation and contrition.

One of the Stations shows Simon of Cyrene helping Jesus to carry the Cross. I once found, in an old magazine at the bottom of a bookcase in our sitting-room, a story about this man – an imaginative human account of a simple man, an onlooker, on his way to market, suddenly caught up in extraordinary events as the soldiers forced him to help Jesus, a convicted criminal staggering under the Cross, lest he die before he reached his destination. The story ended with the moment when Jesus, feeling the weight suddenly lightened, looked back at the ashamed and resentful Simon and smiled in gratitude; and Simon, his life changed by that gratitude, tried to shoulder all the burden.

The story moved me very much; it gave a kind of redemption to the whole bloody scene of the Passion that had been so deeply embedded in our lives, like the coins in the Pin Tree, that we grew around it. We lived with guilt, yet were unable to do much to redeem the guilt, except by not actually doing much. With this Simon one got a chance to feel that humanity was not all wicked, that somewhere there was always one who could help, if only reluctantly, and who might be me or a sister. Until then there had been no leavening in the blackness of humanity. When I had finished reading it, quite laboriously, for I was no more than six or seven, I found that it had been written by my mother.

The Stations of the Cross can be a private devotion, but once a year they constitute a kind of Pilgrim's Progress for the whole district; these services, held each night in October, are attended by great numbers who go as much for the spectacle as for piety, for the Devotions are a theatrical event. The church is lit with candles and a few oil-lamps so that it is full of shadows. The smell and haze of incense floats out from the vestry where one can see the shadowy figures of the priests and altar boys robing but they are always just out of eyeshot here, as they are at the lough shore ceremony. The schoolmaster who plays the old harmonium tests it for wheeze, and the men and women push in through the swing doors, still crossing themselves with the Holy Water from the font in the little outside porch, and still shivering from the night air.

The chapel is strictly divided inside, with all the women to the left of the main aisle and the men on the right and we, the choir, an arbitrary band of children chosen not for voice but availability, upstairs above the women's side. There are no other women in the gallery although the men's gallery opposite is full; it has been known for the priest to stop the service below and bellow up to the younger men and boys to be quiet and 'to quet wrecking' it.

When it is time for the service to begin, the priest and altar boys come out in a procession from the vestry, genuflect in front of the altar and come through the little carved wooden gate in the railings that separate the aisle from the body of the church. Two boys each carry a candelabrum, another carries a censer from which the incense is already smoking up and out and which he swings with considerable flourish: at each Station he reluctantly yields this trophy to the priest who genuflects and swings it. The priest reads out a description of each scene – 'Veronica wipes the face of Jesus', 'Jesus falls the first time', 'Jesus falls the second time.'

It is a magical and mysterious ritual for us children, but I do not feel it is holy, as I feel Benediction is holy, when the Host is revealed on the altar and I hardly dare look. When I read later about how Incas could not look at the face of their king I knew how easily such thaumatolatry could arise, for I never sidled a glance from behind my clasped hands at that white Host held aloft in its sun-burst monstrance without feeling that I would be blinded. It would have been the sin of presumption made manifest, and presumption was a word much used by our teachers – not about our earthly manner and stances, but about our eternal expectations. Those who were presumptuous, by simply relying on God's good graces to see them right, as it were, would certainly be damned.

Anyone happening on our ceremony of the Stations of the Cross from the outside world might have thought they were in Plato's cave or had stumbled on occult, forbidden ceremonies, calling up the darkness in men's hearts rather than celebrating the good: the long flames of candles flickering their light across the priest's face, and the white lace on his vestments highlighting the gold cope and chasuble; the acolyte's censer gleaming as it swung, with each swing a puff of incense drifting up and out like the flies by the lough shore. As the little group of celebrants intone the prayers and responses they move in a sparkling cluster from Station to Station and the congregation turn their bodies to follow. Above the ceremony we chant the hymns that are more like ballads than sacred music, filled with death-wish, expressed with a melancholy energy:

Our fathers chained in prison dark,
Were full of hope and conscience free,
How sweet would be our children's fate
If we like them, could die for you.
Faith of our fathers living still
We will be true to thee till death.

No one would have questioned the sentiment. The priests were constantly exhorting us to fight to the death for our faith, and the continuing process of keeping us enclosed in that faith, barricading us into our moral place, was an obsessional job for priests and educators. In every sermon the outside world was presented as a sinister amphitheatre of evil, of lewd dances and films that were occasions of mortal sin, peopled by determined proselytizers stealthily, inexorably advancing to try to separate us from our faith.

'Ah, children', Father Lappin says, raking us with his wild pale eyes, 'if any one of you would fight Communism with even only half the energy and dedication that each and every Communist brings to his evil desire to lead you to Lucifer, we would defeat it. But we do not, my children, we do not.'

I resolved to fight Communism with my bare hands if necessary, or die nobly like the new young saint Maria Goretti who had resisted to the death the clumsy attempts of a young man to seduce her. Not that we knew why he had killed her. There was no dissembling, no holding back on the number of blows she had been struck or on the details of her death agony, but as to why the young man had battered her to death in a frenzy was a dark mystery only hinted at. 'She would not do what he wished, the vile thing that he wished. She remained pure, pure in the midst of filth and evil, she resisted all attempts on her purity even when struck and struck again.' There were tears in Miss Rogers's eyes as she read out the account from the book on modern martyrs. There were tears in ours; but there were no Communists around waiting to vent their ideological lust and batter us in their frenzy.

Communists had no corporeal shape; they just existed, elementary and awful, and when I tried to visualize them I saw them as not unlike the massed hierarchies of Heaven, waiting and watchful behind the sky. Communists waited, watchful, from behind the Iron Curtain, that heavy barrier suspended God knows how across the map of Europe; one day at some cosmic cue that curtain would rise and then it would be a wailing and gnashing of teeth, especially for us, their truest enemies, whom they would know instinctively at any distance. None of that seemed unreasonable: after all, any one of us knew instinctively when we went outside our territory to Cookstown who was a Protestant and who was a Catholic. And we knew that it worked the other way round. There was nothing magical about it; we operated on tribal signals. But for the moment it was the devil we knew whom we had to fight, and we must never rest in the twenty-four-hour battle that the creatures of darkness waged for our souls.

Lucifer, as we all knew too well, had been God's favourite acolyte and most powerful angel, and there had been an infinitesimal moment when he and God had teetered for ascendancy in the battle of the Firmaments that had ended in the creation of Heaven and Chaos, and the establishment of Pandemonium, the high capital of Satan and his peers; but the battle was continuous, Good and Bad were for ever warring, and there remained always that teetering moment when Bad might win. Each one of us could tip its balance and I still believe it.

There was nothing general and distant about this battle between Lucifer and God, or the Holy Trinity, as God was always spoken of in our theology. It was a most particular struggle waged for each of us, for since Lucifer was perpetually consumed by the twin searing pains of the perpetual loss of love and jealousy of those who still had love, or could have it, we knew that if we tried especially hard to draw near to that good source Lucifer's appetite to have us would be vastly whetted. Lucifer desired us, Miss Rogers explained, to add to his legions so that the battle could always continue; but more, because our loss would cause such anguish to God. I felt that if I could tread the thin line between being moderately good, so that I wasn't a favourite, and moderately bad, so that Lucifer couldn't quite claim me, I would be safer: but I inclined towards being a saint, and moderation, I knew, was lukewarm and I would be vomited out of his mouth. I felt considerable panic at the idea of my cosmic importance in the heavenly scheme, especially as it was so out of kilter with my earthly perceptions of our place and importance.

The sin that most exercised our consciences and imaginations was the sin against the sixth commandment, which was the greatest sin except for the one against the Holy Ghost which we didn't know how to commit either. Not that we wanted to, but you could never be quite sure over which brink of mortal sin you might be teetering, and although we were supposed to be comforted by the knowledge that you had knowingly to commit sin in order for it to gain the status of sin, again, like Bad Thoughts, one never knew where culpability began.

The sixth commandment – 'Thou shalt not covet thy neighbour's wife' – was so astonishingly irrelevant that at first I could not believe it was such a dreadful sin; it seemed to exclude the possibility that any of us, or our mothers or aunts – or indeed any woman – could commit it. Miss Rogers never expounded on it; then Father Lappin explained it as Bad Thoughts, Immodest Touching, Indecent Behaviour and Sins against Chastity. Bad Thoughts was the thing we had most to guard against. The phrase was run together as one word with a special narrow definition, meaning speculations and fantasies and curiosity about sex. What such injunctions, interdicts and strictures did was to make divisions within the confines of our heads, to teach us that there were forbidden territories in our minds, places to be kept at bay. And although thoughts that were labelled 'bad' were supposed to be vanquished or banished by prayer or by the rite of confession, they skulked in a depth of the mind, under a trapdoor, hunkered and hideously shapely, waiting for any weak moment to come pushing up to the surface. Those famous Bad Thoughts which we were so ceaselessly exhorted to resist tumescently haunt many an Irish life.

The Holy Family was our shining example of what the perfect life should be: the ideal woman was the Virgin Mary; the ideal form of fertilization, the Immaculate Conception; the ideal husband, Joseph – a shadowy figure in the interior of his carpenter's shop dressed in flowing garments and looking, in my imagination and indeed in pictorial representations, not unlike the priests as they robed for Mass in the vestry. We girls were representatives of the Blessed Virgin and should at all times try to emulate her behaviour. But there was a built-in failure factor – if we became mothers, we would have to leave her behind as an ideal since we could never achieve a Virgin Birth. Our fairy-stories were of Lazarus dragging his decomposing body from the tomb; the ungrateful lepers, who never returned to say thank-you for their deliverance; the woman who had haemorrhaged for twelve years, and Mary and Martha, especially Mary, who by letting her sister do all the work chose the better part and won all the praise, which seemed manifestly unfair.

Mary, the Holy Mother and Blessed Virgin, standing in utter resignation at the foot of the Cross waiting to receive the battered body of her son, was presented as the perfect role-model; her

130

passivity, her lack of protest, was the only way to greet adversity and evil. Perhaps such absolutes did help women to accept with resignation and humility the many crosses that religion and life laid on them, and certainly there were many truly devout people in the parish who gained comfort from religion, and not just disturbance of their spirit and terrorism and fear. But those two last stalked our childhood in a horrid linkage with righteousness and Christ, and they stalk Northern Ireland still.

And yet many Irish women, for all that they have laboured under such burdens, or perhaps because they have, often possess a goodness and a kind of purity that is rare. In the novel *Langrishe Go Down* by Aidan Higgins, which I believe bears all the hallmarks of truth, the German hero Otto, who has come to live in Ireland, says with fervour: 'Irish women . . . they are so pure and clean. So pure, and that's not to be found any more in Germany, that great purity. But here you have it. And also that look in the face, the eyes, and one knows that such women are not corrupted . . . a man might sometimes have filthy thoughts about girls. That's natural enough. But when I meet Irish girls and can recognize at once their essential purity then I am touched, incapable of a base thought.'

The reverse of this has been that when Irish girls leave Ireland their purity is given another interpretation; it is seen as a pathological condition and becomes merely the expression of a repressed sexuality; just as innocence, viewed in the same light, becomes ignorance. There was for years a tradition and belief, doubtless with a certain foundation, that convent-bred Irish girls were sexually voracious once they were liberated from the restraints of their society.

We were from the earliest age so steeped in the idea that chastity was the highest virtue and that being in a nunnery was a greater vocation than a worldly or sensual life that it was hard to resolve the ambivalences, or to perceive the denial of our selves that this *modus vivendi* entailed. It was a way of life based on a dark and frightful ambiguity; women were viewed both as powerful creatures, stained with Pauline and liturgical descriptions of them as darkling female stews, potent potential occasions of sin, and as inferior beings, domestic creatures, with no effective life apart

131

from motherhood and wifehood. The fear of sex, the forbidden-ness of any pleasure in sex, was deeply interwoven with our teachings. The same priests and nuns who read out, 'There is no fear in love: but perfect love casteth out fear because fear hath torment. He that feareth is not made perfect in love,' presented the whole issue of human love to us as something darkly morbid, so covered in moral pitch that even to think of it was to risk being besmirched.

We were taught that we were fashioned in the image of God and thus were fit vessels to receive Him, alive and well in the form of the sanctified Host at Communion; yet in the same lesson we were taught that these same bodies were tabernacles of sin, the source of unspeakable passions and uncleanliness. We never openly questioned such discrepancies or mysteries since we were also taught that by doing so we were questioning the very edifice of our faith. Mysteries are an absolute part of our faith, inexplicable and irrational and lying heavy and morose at the heart of our religion.

'What do you mean by a mystery?' Father O'Hare, the curate who has come into our classroom to examine us, to see if we are fit to receive our First Communion, flings the question from the front of the class to the back. Miss Rogers tries to divert it by sheer force of will towards those she thinks may be able to answer him. Those of us who know the answer (although we have no idea of its meaning) chant it in confident unison: 'Please Father, by a mystery I mean a truth which is above reason but revealed by God.'

'Is the Holy Mass one and the same Sacrifice?' We knew about sacrifice and its meaning and its reality. From earliest childhood we had been taught to offer up our sufferings as sacrifices. Any thwarting of desire, any frustrations, any unfairnesses, any hard-ships or disappointments could be made all to the good, if we would but offer them silently to God. And we contrived sacrifices too, giving up sweets in Lent, walking when we wanted to run and remembering St Brendan who, it was reputed, abandoned the letter 'O' in mid-stroke when he heard his superior calling him, so perfect was his obedience. We rather thought that if any of us laid down our pens with such a nice obedience we might be accused of clock-watching or lack of enthusiasm for the job in hand. And with every sacrifice we remembered the ultimate one, held up before us night and day – the lacerated, tortured, naked Jesus on the Cross.

'Yes, the Holy Mass is one and the same sacrifice with that of the Cross, inasmuch as Christ, who offered himself a bleeding victim on the Cross, continues to offer himself in an unbloody manner on the altar through the ministry of his priests.'

'What is the Holy Eucharist?' Father O'Hare moves nearer to the front row of desks.

'The sacrament of the Holy Eucharist is the true Body and Blood of Jesus Christ together with his Soul and Divinity under the appearance of bread and wine.'

Priest and teacher beam. We have passed the test and can certainly receive First Communion. Thirty years later I looked up the meaning of that word Eucharist, embedded so deeply in my word-store that I had never thought of it as having a meaning at all. It means the giving of thanks, gratitude.

Eiram, Morgan and I made our First Communion, or we 'received the Sacrament', as it is called, on the same day. In the commemorative photograph we are all three wearing short white net veils attached under our chins by elastic, and look like fairly unwilling participants in a parody of bridal ritual. The Catholic church knows all there is to know about ceremony and magic initiation rites, and their central function in our human lives.

Eiram's knuckles are clenched. Morgan's hands are clasped across her silk sash. Our dresses are white, with long sleeves, and all three of us are very conscious of the fact that Jesus has just entered us. Not for nothing are we attired as brides. I feel that an aura of holiness, a bodily halo must surround us; I, who could never look at the Exposition of the Host at Benediction in case something shattered, was very put about to have to receive the same Host on my tongue. I feared that in trying to swallow it, I would choke.

Of all the sisters Morgan seemed the most affected by the ritual and outward forms of religion. Indeed at times she appeared to be afflicted by that psychological ailment that nuns and student priests are heir to and are warned against, an over-scrupulousness of conscience in which the slightest deviation from some prescribed course of action appears to be a major breach of the rules. Those who suffer from this encroachment of scruple seem increasingly to need to introduce rules and limits and patterns into their lives, to keep the chaos of life at bay.

Each night she knelt at the side of her bed in the little room behind my parents' room where she and Sinclare and I slept. Sinclare had to go to bed earlier, being younger, and she lay boring a hole through the wall with a finger whose nail was worn down and permanently white-tipped by the small silent scrapings through mortar and plaster. Like a creature in a fairy-story or a fable she scratched towards the other side where Ellen lay, and every night the little conical hole got deeper. Sinclare's eyes were so large and round that they reminded people of kittens' eyes; they gave her face a startled look and her voice had the same quality, rising higher as she talked or told a story, so that even commonplace things appeared astounding since they invariably ended up on high C.

There was always an oil-lamp on the dressing-table, and on winter nights it was kept lit and turned down low. One night I climbed on to the table, turned the wick up and burned a book by holding each page across the small glass globe. Sinclare watched me, her eyes expanding even more and her voice becoming a squeak that only incited me further. When my mother found the charred pages the next morning she stood very still and it was through this unexpected silence – for she was normally voluble – that I realized what I might have done.

Each night Morgan pressed her hands together – the most beautiful hands in the family, pale and smooth (indeed everything about her is shapely and smooth, her hair, her face, her body and the little white gleaming half-moons at the bottom of her nails) – and anxiously began her prayers. If anyone interrupted her at any point she had to start all over again and, since her prayers seemed endless, and our patience was none too long, we nearly always did interrupt. We were fundamentally sympathetic and understood the talismanic significance of reaching the end of the long intercessions with God without interruption. But we each had our own rituals, our own way of conducting life and imposing order on it, and we never expected sisterly co-operation. Indeed most of us anticipated the opposite, and were as rough in our justice towards Morgan.

Every night each one of us prayed silently the prayer that we had been taught in school: the Act of Contrition. 'Oh my God I am heartily sorry for having offended thee and I detest sin above every other evil, because it offends thee my God Who Art worthy of all my love and I firmly resolve by Thy Holy Grace never more to offend thee and to amend my life. Amen.' Then we prayed the prayer that guaranteed we would never die in our sleep, or die unawares, and climbed into bed and crossed our arms over our chest as a surefire way of gaining an indulgence. We did not seek indulgences for ourselves, but for all those who had had the misfortune to be born outside the Catholic fold. We were taught daily to thank God for the inestimable privilege of being born a Catholic, a blessing and privilege that the rest of the world would give its eye-teeth for. 'The luck, the gift, girls, the blessing of being born into the only one true faith,' Miss Rogers marvelled. 'Whatever else happens to you, no matter what you do or don't do, remember that *more* will always be expected of you since you started out with more, and must account for it at the end.' Stones under the saddle, as it were, before the race of life.

It was granted non-Catholics, as they were always termed, might be saved if they had led as good a life as possible in view of their benighted circumstances. We were extremely relieved by this caveat, since it meant our cousin Maurice, who lived in Warrenpoint and whom I loved with a passion that persisted, and whom the fishermen with their predilection for nicknames called 'Whiteskull' as soon as they saw his silver-blond hair, would not be banished to burn in Hell for all eternity, but would only be temporarily incarcerated, although burning, in Purgatory.

'Do you remember', Morgan asked me once, 'when we were very small, how you found me crying behind the hayshed in the haggart? I told you it was because of my bad thoughts and I didn't know what to do?' It was at the end of a long conversation about the coil that sisters are tied in; from her tone I knew that the hour was vivid in her mind, the quality of the day, her despair, my

135

presence. From my shaky vantage-point of a year older, the world seemed always to have been shouting of sin and morality at Morgan and I was fearful for her, but fearful of her too. I minded this more than I let myself know, because of that law in the hierarchy of sisters that the older must always inspire awe or fear – never the other way around.

So although I do not remember that afternoon in the haggart behind the hayshed when stars were shining out of sight and Morgan told me of her fear of her thought-sins, I can too easily relive others when I was crying myself, lying in the silver lichened branches of a fallen tree in a small triangle of land hidden by ditches, which was the secret place, where no one would find me. The truth was that no one was looking, and eventually I would rise up from the crook of the tree, and the moss, and the beetles which had begun to roam over me, and resentful of the lack of alarums over my disappearance go back into life, plotting revenge or seeking succour, or both.

It is odd that I do not remember Morgan's attempt to get help with her religious pain, since given our habitual defences it must have been a rare appeal on her part; but she had cause to believe that I could help her as I had tried to turn myself into her guardian. If I had not done so I would have tried to destroy her. One of the salient things about Morgan was the enchanting effulgence of her face, incandescent with goodwill. When she smiled her face switched on. After Barry-Paul was born when she was three her expression changed subtly and a stricken look entered her face. The significance of the arrival of a male had percolated to her; she approached our mother feeding her newborn son and asked, 'Am I still your little girl?' Our mother, perhaps locked into a moment of pain of her own, or simply harassed, answered, 'Oh give my head peace.'

We all choose our moments to ask such questions and we choose our answers, even in heat and tiredness, so that they will reverberate in a certain way: as my mother ruefully recognized. For it is she who tells the story years later and who recognizes, dearly enough, what happened that day and who in telling the story hopes perhaps to drain that sump, to draw the poison, to gain redemption for her response.

'A child doesn't ask a question like that twice,' she said wearily to Nell, her youngest daughter, who holds her own daughter the tighter.

13

Our priests were the most powerful people in the parish and they ruled their little kingdoms like despots, frowning on anything that might weaken their civil as well as their priestly and absolute authority. Like many priests of that epoch they were well-meaning men of narrow and bigoted education, with no families of their own to temper their received, fixed and narrow ideas; they were often overbearing and impatient in judgement, but their authority was never questioned. Father Lappin, the parish priest, was a rather remote figure since he lived up in Mullinahoe, on the far side of the aerodrome; and with his wild white eyes he looked like the enchanted human from the Coleridge poem we had lately learnt,

. . . Beware! Beware!
His flashing eyes, his floating hair!
Weave a circle round him thrice,
And close your eyes with holy dread,
For he on honey-dew hath fed,
And drunk the milk of Paradise.

Father O'Hare, his curate, who drove dangerously about the countryside in an old car on his own mysterious errands, had red hair and a scarlet face and a fiery choleric temper. He assaulted small girls in the classroom under the guise of stroking or cuddling them, and those who suffered his attacks could never speak of it. It was all done innocently enough, and I think no adult, not even the priest, really recognized what was happening. Even the child who suffered it could never admit it, not even to herself, since it was not believable.

Both the parish priest and curate were deeply concerned, not to say obsessed, with money, understandably enough since there were very few parish fund-raising activities to pay their stipends, never mind keep the church standing, and they often spoke of little else at the Sunday sermon except how to make ends meet. The main stipends came from the quarterly dues collected by a representative of each townland. The contributions were read out at Mass, from little red books filled with the names of the heads of households; the only women who contributed separately were the two schoolteachers. We settled back in our pews disconsolately as the priest reached behind him for the first of the high stack of books, and if it was Father Lappin reading the lists the congregation gave a perceptible groan, since his sermons and readings could take up to an hour, as he lingered over the odious litany of names.

'Anneeterberg,' he intoned. 'Paddy Kelly – four shillings. Tommy Coyle – five shillings. Peter Mahon – two and sixpence. James Haggan – two and sixpence. John Bradley – two shillings.'

On most Sundays there was a copper collection, when pennies were dropped into the long-handled boxes pushed along the pews; but once a month there was the silver collection, and on such days the priest celebrating Mass would take off his alb, come down from the altar and walk around behind a man chosen from the congregation who knew everyone's name, and who holding out the collecting-plate would whisper to the priest what each person had given. The priest then repeated it loudly. It was a hateful practice, turning the church into a market place, but it was an effective one.

There were stories connected with Father Flanagan, the parish priest who had been the incumbent immediately before Father Lappin, and this silver collection. Father Flanagan had become legendary because of his cruel tongue, bad temper and the arbitrary way in which he would suddenly berate a parishioner in confession or at a collection; the two most famous occasions each caused a sensation in the parish and their repercussions reverberated through conversation and memory for years afterwards. Indeed, one of these occasions had caused his downfall.

The first sensation had occurred one Sunday when the silver

collection was being taken up; Tamsie had been chosen to accompany Father Flanagan on his rounds of the pews and he happened on that rare creature, a stranger in the chapel, who put a pound note in the plate. Tamsie leaned over bashfully and asked his name and the stranger, perhaps shy or, as might seem more likely, appalled by the barbaric practice of an auction taking place in the house of God, shook his head and would not answer. Father Flanagan was staring at the pound. 'A friend', Tamsie the collector announced with great presence of mind, 'one pound.' There was a rustle in the church. The sum was unprecedented. The man next to him, an inhabitant of the parish, gave his half-crown – and as Tamsie, who regaled us with the story, observed, 'Hard enough it was for him to find the half-crown to give in the first place.' Before Tamsie could announce his name the priest interrupted: 'A far-out friend,' he jeered, triumphant at his own humiliating wit. But the parish never forgave him and when, some years later, the sermon scandal occurred and Feley got him his comeuppance, feeling was all on Feley's side. There was too a certain amount of grim pleasure taken in the fact of two such mighty pillars of the parish as Father Flanagan and Philomena Rogers simultaneously crashing, the one being pulled down in the other's fall.

Philomena Rogers was one of the wise women of the parish, foremost in that tribe of older women who waited attendance on the priest, looked after the vestry and the priests' vestments, polished the hanging brass sacramental lamp that was hoisted up and down on an elaborate pulley over the altar, washed the altar linen, replaced the candles, and – if there were any flowers available in the parish – arranged them on the altar. These women attended daily Mass and made outward show of all kinds of religious observance including confession every Saturday – although no one could imagine why, save through excess of scruple. Although such women were privately somewhat ridiculed for their ostentatious show of religiosity, and their actual degree of piety was occasionally doubted, they were, all the same, above reproach.

One Sunday when Father Flanagan was preaching about honesty and hypocrisy he stood at the altar, strangely silent for a man with such a waspish tongue, lost for a moment as he searched for a devastating simile.

'The man who says he is pious and honest, my dear brethren', he said, 'and yet does not do an honest day's work for an honest day's pay, has as much good in him . . .' – he stopped, and his congregation, bemused perhaps at the idea of an honest day's work being available at all, waited to hear how he would convey the moral turpitude of such a person – '. . . has as much good in him as – as Philomena Rogers.'

There was a perfect, appalled silence, as the words echoed and pealed throughout the church.

'As much good in him as Philomena Rogers.' There was a choking noise from the women's side of the church and Philomena got up, pulled her shawl over her head, and ran out. The congregation, frozen by disbelief, was released into astonishment by her flight, released into a whispering coughing exclamatory confusion not unmixed with a certain anticipatory delight. The priest stood still at the altar, stunned by his slip, aware of the enormity of what he had done. He blessed himself and turned back to the altar and finished the Mass as best he could. The congregation filed out hardly looking at each other, and my father drove home utterly shocked, unable, he said, to credit what he had heard. He had just got in the door when he saw Philomena's brother, Feley, hurrying around the gable of the house.

'Were you at the eight o'clock Mass?' he asked. His body was shaking. My father made him sit down. 'Did he say what she said he said from the altar?' Feley asked. 'Is Philomena's head away with it at the heel of the hunt, or is she making it, or what?'

'She's not making it,' my father said. 'He did say it. He forgot himself, or he lost his head or something. But listen', he said, trying to calm Feley, who looked as though he would do himself harm, 'don't pay attention. Nobody will pay any heed to what happened. The priest is hasty, we all know that. He didn't know what he was saying, he said the first thing that came into his head.'

'And by Christ', Feley said, 'it'll be the last, for I'll have the greath off the guilderhead fornenst it.' His dark skin seemed stretched across his bones with rage and pain. We watched him

140

with fascinated horror from the settle, as he rocked back and forth.

The greath was a kind of harness used to keep a horse correctly positioned within the shafts of a cart, and a guilderhead was someone so stupid and clumsy as to be despised and avoided. Feley carried out his threat. He hired a driver to take him to Armagh where the Cardinal Bishop lived and within a week Father Flanagan had been removed from the parish and Father Lappin had arrived.

But by far the most sensational religious event in the annals of the parish occurred in the autumn of 1954, long after Father Flanagan's time. A pious woman of the parish, the mother of eight children and therefore, it was supposed, not easily given to hysteria or religious mania, was reputed to have seen a vision of the Virgin Mary standing in a black-thorn tree near the new council cottages at Anneetermore, the first council houses to be built in the lower parish since the two little ones were built near the Old Cross in 1929.

Anneetermore – the name means 'large forested field' – lies two miles on the other side of the school from us and thus it was foreign territory; we only saw it from the car when our mother or father drove us down to be measured for a dress or skirt by the dressmaker who lived beyond it. It was a small new housing-estate, and the planning that went into it was minimal and uncaring; the houses were built from the cheapest possible blue-print and materials, with no regard for local customs or modes. Their great advantage was that they had indoor lavatories and bathrooms. They were two-storied, square, finished in dingy rend-ered cement and built in pairs, with each pair divided from the next only by a fence of low wire-netting. In a society where people were obsessively secretive about themselves, and equally curious about other people's business, the new proximities in the cottages were alarming. Everything was on view, and the ancient tensions between some transplanted families became aggravated and flared into frequent fights – so much so that during the period of adjustment the place became known as Little Korea. Because of the alien look of these houses built so symmetrically in one place, and the number of children who lived in them, I thought of

Anneetermore with an envious but frightened fascination, as a child living in the quiet, genteel suburb of a town, for example, might yearn over the apparently vivacious aspect of a crowded slum.

Anneetermore seemed an odd enough place for the Blessed Virgin to make her appearance; but Lourdes or Fatima, the great shrines to her earthly visitations, were not after all very prepossessing. Ever since I had sunk into holy rapture at a showing of the sentimental film about Lourdes, *The Song of Bernadette*, in a cinema in Stewartstown some twenty miles away, I had scanned the skies, eyes like radar, hoping to see the Virgin clad in pale blue wafting towards me, or ensconced in a cloud accompanied by a smell of lilies, smiling down on me. Now it appeared Bridie had seen her first, and I was put out, as though there had been a cosmic error of timing and identity. Reports about subsequent sightings were hazy (it was always a friend of a friend), and the priests never mentioned it, in keeping with the laissez-faire policy of the church on matters of visions and apparitions; the occurrence would either be forgotten after the customary seven days' wonder, or would have enough substance to withstand the attrition of time and investigation. The tacit disapproval of the clerical establishment did not stop thousands of people from all over Ireland and parts of Europe flocking to the cottages hoping to be vouchsafed a glimpse of the Madonna. I was among them, the fervent hopeful.

It was a bright moonlight night when I set out with Ellen and Mary-Jane to walk the four miles to Anneetermore. Elizabeth and Eiram were at boarding-school, and Morgan was too small to be included in the outing. She and Sinclaré were already in bed in our room when I left the house with Ellen and Mary-Jane, almost ill with excitement, anticipation and a certain guilt since I felt my parents disapproved of the whole thing. They rather shared the official attitude.

Bridie, the woman who was reputed to have seen the vision, was Mary-Jane's sister, and I felt that this kinship might give us some kind of exclusivity, a spiritual entrée. But as we passed the chapel, over a mile away from the new cottages, the crowds were already enormous. The narrow road was jammed with bicycles and people trying to get nearer to the site, and parked cars further obstructed our passage. The crowds were almost silent: occasionally someone would shout a name, trying to locate a child missing in the darkness; a young girl would giggle, a man would whistle a bar of music and then fall silent as though afraid of irreverence. Everyone was preoccupied with trying to inch nearer to the putative site, as it drew closer to the time at which the Virgin was supposed to have first made her appearance. As we were borne along I dreaded losing Mary-Jane and Ellen, dreaded being separated from them in the enormous dense crowd; but we held together until the river of people was dammed to a stop by the immovable block of the crowds already on the site some distance from the cottages. No one could go any further. I was standing on the bank at the side of the road squashed between Mary-Jane and Ellen and above me was a sycamore tree with two children already lodged in the branches. I joined them and sat astraddle a branch looking at the extraordinary tumult of heads below. All the bodies were pressed tightly together, every face was turned upwards anticipating, scanning. Gradually all talking stopped until it seemed as if a canopy of silence had been laid over the crowded heads.

A woman with a loud high voice began to recite the Rosary and the crowd chanted the response to the Hail Mary. When the long incantations had finished, the silence pressed in again. A woman screamed, and at the sudden hysterical sound the mass of people quivered and rustled and murmured as though connected, the sound like wind rippling over barley. Above the swaying heads, an arm suddenly semaphored and I strained in the direction of the pointing fingers.

I longed to see her with her mild put-upon face and red roses pinned into her feet but I could see nothing.

Again someone shrieked an imploration, the crowd moaned in response and shivered as one body, and another woman, with a high, frantic, piercing voice, or perhaps the same one who had begun the Rosary, began to sing – or to bewail – a hymn; the crowd joined in: the hymn swelled powerfully over the roofs of the houses, the sound full of an enormous, desperate emotion. The air was so moist with it that I felt the dew of prayer would settle on my shoulders and gleam on the leaves of the sycamore around me. When the hymn ended there was an unstill silence. The crowd lost its powerful unity and collapsed into separate units, coughing and stamping its feet, and began to move outwards from the scene where something had happened but no one knew what. Car headlights were switched on, spotlighting individual dazed faces, as though the audience who thought they had been viewing something with an intense vision, boring through darkness to a drama of their own making, were suddenly revealed to each other and themselves as the actors in the drama and not spectators; they found, too, that the action departed with them.

I climbed down from the tree and joined Ellen and Mary-Jane; we pushed our way on to the road and started with the tide of people for the Kiln Corner and thence towards home. The sound now was of engines and talk and coughing, overwhelming, ordinary noise. I did not yet know whether there had been a vision which I had not merited. Ellen spoke. Her voice was full of anxiety and scepticism and suspicion. 'Did yous see anything?' I shook my head into the darkness. 'The child didn't see a hait', Mary-Jane said, 'no more than any of us, for there was nothing to see. It's all a mock.'

Her robust assertion was astonishing to me. It was a living illustration of the story of the Emperor's new clothes. I recognized it as such and something shifted in that place where I still so rigidly kept my faith. It was also my first glimpse of the power of auto-suggestion and mass hysteria; I saw how easy it was to want to believe, to be certain.

That little shift was the most frightening thing I had ever felt. Years later, among the legends about the *Titanic*, I came on an anecdote told by a survivor of how one man at a table with other revellers had felt a shudder, or shiver, in the ship. 'What was that?' he asked, and a companion said casually: 'It was a bump. I felt a bump.' 'A bump?' the questioner said. 'A bump in the middle of the ocean?' And in his own question he heard the meaning of what had been said and what he was asking, its implication of something unbelievable, enormous and final. But I kept such bumps to myself; to have confessed would have meant recognizing what had happened, and that was still far beyond me. It was an unnameable thing and if I had recognized it I would certainly have had to confess it, because not confessing something one knew was sinful was the third terrible sin: Making A Bad Confession.

All children over the age of seven attended the monthly confession held on Saturday mornings – rows of us waiting in the pews outside the confessional. There was a green half-door in the priest's compartment topped by two green curtains through which he looked out at us as we waited to be shriven, and since the doors of the confessional cubicles did not quite reach the top we all feared that the sound of our sins would drift out to the scandalized ears of the other children. Once inside one of the mock-Gothic cubicles on each side of the priest's lair we knelt, guilty, waiting for the child in the other cubicle to finish her tale of woe, at which point the priest would push the shutter back from the grid and tilt his head towards one's own whisper. Afterwards, when the catalogue of crime had been delivered to the priest, and there had been scrupulous heart-searching about whether or not you could remember any other sins, he gave you a penance. It was always Three Hail Mary's, which took less than a minute to say, and then we were out of the chapel and into the open air liberated as larks, souls soaring at peace with the world. Until my transgression, when my guilt returned, engorged on new sin, I always felt my face must be transfigured.

I was frightened of priests, as indeed most children in the parish were; and part of this fear stemmed from the knowledge that our adults feared them too. As a social system – which it was – our religion constituted a tyranny. There was no defence against them, nor avoidance of their religious authority, since objections to their modes and methods and interference was seen merely as subversive and sinful, and any criticism was labelled anti-clerical, which was commonly supposed to be a sin. Indeed any criticism, however rational, was taken as a wicked personal affront, and even the most logical and well-meaning attempts to broaden the inbred form of our Catholicism were treated as the thin end of a large wedge, a hatchet-attack on the whole institution. Since forgiveness for such a heinous crime could only be gained by confessing, in all probability to the priest whom you had criticized, discretion tended to prevail.

But even though they wielded such absolute authority they were figures from which we could escape, swirling as they did in and out of our lives in arbitrary irregular ways. There was no escape from the nuns I found myself under when I went to join Elizabeth and Eiram at convent boarding-school. They ruled us from morning to night, burning so with their own inner authority, their own certainty that they had chosen the best path through life, that anything other than great respect and fear was rare in their presence. Even such a small untidiness as a piece of their hair not quite tucked behind the starched white coifs that framed their faces, giving them a curious intense whiteness and a detached purity, was unhinging to their image rather than humanizing.

After two years I left boarding-school to go to a convent day-school; the boarding-school became in retrospect and by contrast, a free and easy paradise. The nuns in the order that ran the day-school had a narrowness of outlook and apparent evaporation of earthly expectation, emotion, or fulfilment that gave all their faces a pinched, curdled look. They walked briskly, their heavy black skirts swirling, their hands tucked under the stationary blast of the scapular that fell from under the white wimple at their neck, back and front, to the hems of their skirts, their rosary beads making a faint rattling as they moved. The alarums of their gait seemed to suggest they were about to happen on the committing of some sin, and the spaces around their black-clad bodies were filled with an emanation of their gauntness, so that before you saw them or, even earlier, heard their rustling, rattling approach, you felt a precursory cold ooze.

Looking at their faces, their skin strained so tautly that not only was all excess flesh and emotion skimmed off, but kindness and humour and appreciation of variety too, I could only wonder at what processes, what abnegation of self had been involved in so successful yet so sour a rendering-down. I speculate now on whether the particular order of nuns attracted aspirants of a certain cast of mind and body, or whether they started off like any other eighteen-year-olds, eager novices burning to offer themselves as Brides of Christ, and only when arrayed in these particular veils and habits began to hone themselves for God. They seemed, in their attitude to us in their charge and care, not only to have

146

abandoned all that was fruitful and sensuous in their natures but to regard such attributes with horror; as though any admission or appreciation of them would mean defection and sin. The nourishments of love were missing. Yet they pursued the course of their lives in the name of Love, they had no other motive than the pursuit of Love, they lived their days in verbal adoration of Love. The paradoxes inherent in their system of living seemed insoluble to me.

They dressed in anachronistic ways as though taking part in a costume drama, revelling in the antiquation of their ways, using clothes to make serious statements about themselves, their obedience and chastity, drawing on the experience of their celibate withdrawal to teach us how best to conduct our sap-filled lives. They were full of advertisement about who they were, whilst preaching retirement and discretion. If loving your neighbour as yourself is the greatest virtue, then the evidence of self-loathing that they ceaselessly paraded boded no good for us, who were both their neighbours and their children (for it is one of the arguments for celibacy among the nuns and clergy that by forfeiting children of their own they may devote themselves more fully to children in their charge). Sometimes I felt we were being punished for existing when their own children did not. There can be few children educated in convent schools who have not got one, or many, stories to tell about particular nuns which reveal an almost unnatural bitterness and antagonism towards the young females in their charge.

When I was adolescent and boarding in their care, I once decided not to go to evening Devotions in the school chapel. I had been to Mass that day and Devotions were not compulsory. There were only five cubicled bathrooms among the fifty girls in our dormitory and since there were always queues I decided to take a bath while the dormitories were empty. Uneasily I climbed into the bath and was scarcely submerged in the water, which I had laboriously run over my hand to deaden the sound, when I heard a nun coming up the stairs. I can still feel the chill that came out of my body. I crouched in the bath with my guilt, my fear, and my despairing knowledge that in any breach of a rule, however minimal, I should always be found out. Mingled with my terror was shame – shame of my body, shame at being found naked, shame at the sybarism of an unhurried bath. She came into the big room with its cubicles of bathrooms, and I could hear her flinging open the doors, rattling closed handles. She came to mine. The water froze around me. The handle moved. 'Who is in there?' Her soft voice was full of pleasure. 'Come out of there, whoever's in there.' I rose. The towel was too small. I could not dry myself quickly enough. I threw the clothes on my wet body and came out, and she pulled me by the arms triumphantly, and shouted at me of sin and mortality. Yet she expected me and all my sisters to call her sister.

There seemed no reasonable way we could connect with these men and women who were our mentors, our exemplars, our guides to life and maturity, who thought of themselves as the brides and grooms of Christ, who directed us so assiduously down life-diminishing paths and who taught us, through the goodness of their hearts, a perverted doctrine: that the beautiful was suspect, that sensuality was a sin, that to deny the good things on earth was admirable, that offering up these denials as sacrifice was praiseworthy, and most of all that Christianity and charity were based solely on savage and bloody events, and not on a great prophet's great teachings. They were trained to forge order, not to admit doubt, and it is a pity that their order so often contributed to so many small children crying desolately over their prayers at night, small children who, when they grew up and became fathers and mothers themselves, were often still desolate and crying.

14

It was books that began to show me a way out, although I was persuaded that even finding such a route to reality was probably bordering on sin, especially as Father Lappin constantly exhorted us to be on our guard against the written word. It was not just that the devil had all the best tunes, he also had control over the printing presses of the world. There was hardly a book since the Book of Kells that Father Lappin did not look on with frightful suspicion.

Our mother had always tried to counteract the effect of our place and time and teaching, to give us access to a more normal life, to give us enough equipment to lead the ordinary contemporary life she knew lay just outside our present boundaries. She made great efforts to have us listen to music other than the ballads and threnodies of the district that we heard in the neighbouring houses or floating out from the pub at night. She tried too to get us suitable reading-matter, but we lived many miles from any bookshop – and there were few books to be had after the war. 'She did manage to get some though,' Eiram said. 'She scoured Belfast to get *Wings of Courage* by George Sand, which made a terrific impact on me – the story of Clopinel and the old ornithologist. He dies in the end; it ends, "Adieu good folks have no trouble for me I have found my wings again." The impact of that. It was my first brush with poetry.'

We could sometimes abandon the reality of our lives through reading, but we rarely lost ourselves in others' fictive imaginings, for our world was too daily, too palpably with us to be readily displaced. The books, other than the ones which lay in the loft, which had the most effect on my imaginative life were those sent once a year by an aunt, a half-sister of my mother's, a nun and the headmistress of a girls' convent school outside Los Angeles. They were the Year Books of Palos Verdes School. These books had the imprimatur of goodness on them. They were Catholic volumes, from a place that existed, but I read them as despatches from a dream world. They shoved images into my head and heart like wedges, prising them open, and they revealed as no other books had ever done that a different parallel world to ours existed, and, what was more, that had an approved existence.

These books had the impact of archives from the future, since the materials and lay-out used in them were then to us rare and exotic. They were bound in a padded synthetic leather that was as luxurious and strange as a mink pelt might have been to an Elizabethan, and their pages were coated with a shiny finish. The

149

nun, sending a quick signal to her half-sister, our mother, also a teacher, to show her what *her* school life involved, could surely never have imagined the startling effect those books would have had on her half-sister's children. Their fat vinyl covers pulsated, for me at least, with the kind of life contained within the spongey fungoid softness of a mushroom. My hands tingled holding them, as though holding the germ of alibi. Their extraordinary secret, the important salient thing about them, was that they were true. The world they described was real, although it had no reality. There was no point of contact between the girls in the books and me, except our common age.

These sunny golden girls who suddenly assumed life as I opened the albums had another separate life from the one I endowed them with. They were contemporaries on another side of the world, and here were their names below their photographs, ordinary recognizable Christian names made strange and foreign by the Italian or Jewish or German surnames they bore, as well as other glittering names like Cindy, and Lou-Anne, and Sherry. And there were other marvellous eccentricities, like using for first names the ones that were familiar to us only as surnames. The commonplace name of Kelly or Donovan became infinitely glamorous when the order was reversed. I can remember most of those names today, in a litany that reverberated in my head and mingled in a voluptuous resonance with the litanies that we chanted in church. Gail Baumgold, Patricia Froebel, Jo-Ann Paticky-Stein, Anna Maria Barberino, Lois Jacovelli, Alex Mirabella, Kelly Bardin, became as one with House of Gold, Tower of Ivory, Ark of the Covenant and Morning Star. Those who possessed the secular names seemed as strange and fabulous as unicorns, and their pursuits were equally amazing. They glee-clubbed, joined sororities, were cheer-leaders, played for pennants and had class pins and rings. As each Year Book arrived I followed the progress and careers of certain girls moving upwards through the school, as an earth-bound scientist might chart the progress of Icarus. No matter if they had waxy wings and the Californian sun was near; by the time they fell they would be out of my sight and for me they were always soaring. I gazed at their sunny golden faces, at their luxuriantly open expressions bearing so unguardedly down

150

on the camera, and wondered how such expressions had been arrived at. The minds behind them, I thought, had not had to learn that they were worthless, like chaff in the wind. I stared appalled and entranced at the enormous long felt skirts buoyed out by petticoats, the cap-sleeved blouses, under which one could see, quite plainly, cantilevered pointing twin bosoms, the tiny swimming-costumes, fur-edged hoods, shorts and T-shirts which fitted closely to their bodies, and I knew with a misplaced certainty that these girls did not wait helplessly for life to arrive at them from some time in the future. They walked towards it, indeed planned for it.

Our ingrained superstition would have excluded such forward planning, had it not already been excluded by the inbred lack of expectation, the discrimination, the injunctions not to tamper with the whim of a fiery God who held your future in his jealous hand. These girls seemed to take a measure of control of their own destinies as a matter of course, and had so many choices, from the profound to the trivial. It was in the trivia that I found most cause for wonderment. They voted on the girl most likely to succeed, or the most popular girl, or the girl most likely to go to Hollywood; such frivolity was obviously condoned by those who taught them since it was printed in these books.

Then, too, there was the fact that books to us had always constituted a substantial but remote world in themselves; for us books *were*, existing only as finished objects passed from one generation to another. Our schoolbooks had been used by children who were now parents themselves. The idea of a printed book having a tendril connection with oneself, of having had a hand in the book's making, with a photograph, a list of one's own ambitions, hobbies, preoccupations, was not within our conception. And yet these girls, like us, were being educated by nuns – that was the most amazing intelligence of all.

I sometimes thought that if I had been able to send a Year Book of our lives back to Palos Verdes, its photographs and text might have had the same haunting fascination for them that those semblances of us children in front of the Cross preserved in early photographs have for me now. I gaze at our images, bodies hunched as though bearing too much knowledge, acquired too early, about what the world had in store, and I look away impotent, perturbed by perceiving their sorrow so candidly. There may not be any sorrow, perhaps it is only my grieved imagination that is staining them, my own retrospection, my interpretation of that vanished and now unknowable world, just as my imagination and longing may have endowed those Los Angeles girls' faces with happiness. Memory is so biased, retaining only what it chooses, recalling the incident that will bolster the idea you need to have to retain your current idea of yourself, distorting incidents to give your past the particular significance you have already endowed it with, as an explanation for your sense of grievance, your reactions, your strange ways of love and especially perhaps your search for consolation. Some of us remember most vividly pain; others remember happiness; others, tears. We all, every child in the family, remember all three, in a different order at different times.

But I thought then that those girls could surely reconcile their inner world with their outer one, and that the one was not necessarily in danger from the other; that fright, subterfuge, evasion and constant defensiveness need not be an intrinsic part of youth. I wanted to despise their world, its surface charm, its plasticity, but I dreamt of it at night. It was a healthy, funny, open, colourful, vivid world, where to be young was not a crying shame; and it was very far away.

15

One hot still July day when the boats were all out and the graveyard was deserted save for the watcher with the spy-glasses up on the Point keeping a look-out for King, Eiram and I slid down the secret path to the shore to be about our business. She was skimming stones over the water and counting the triumphant skims when there was, sudden, amazing, an invasion.

Down the lower path which skirts the Cross and graveyard

comes a crocodile of children neatly dressed and carrying baskets, the procession headed by a Vicar. We are put out to see a man in a dog-collar wearing grey clothes and not the black of our priests, but it is the shiny neat children, so precise, so beautifully uniform, that hold us. They might have been a dragoon of Hussars clattering past the sloe-trees from the way we stare. A Sunday School outing. We have never seen so many shiny children before, although I have met individual children like them, friends of my aunt and uncle who live in Warrenpoint. This town has an enormous fascination for me, partly as a place of excavation of my mother's past, partly because it is so utterly different from where we live, and partly because so many apocalyptic events take place there in my young life; because I suppose I have ventured out of my own territory and am subject to chance and change. It was in Warrenpoint that I first perceived Eiram as another person; and in Warrenpoint I commit sin.

It is a pretty Edwardian seaside town, with bay-windowed boarding-houses, a proper sea-front with breakwaters and boats for hire and bandstand and a large open air salt-water swimming-bath painted white and green with cabins and canopies and high white railing jutting out into the sea. It is utter, utter glamour. Part of this glamour comes from the aunt with whom I stay, my mother's sister; she is witty, humorous, with plenty of time, and her slender blonde body is quite unlike the bodies of women at home – hers looks like that of a young girl and she wears swimsuits and tailored suits. She treats me with delicacy and love, and I respond with such a passion that, although I crave home, I long to stay with her: her son Maurice – 'Whiteskull' – is my first real sexually-based love and I observe his life with an astonished curiosity. But the other people we meet there seem alien, especially the children, and it is through them that the first intimation that we are inferior is subtly brought home to me.

These children are casually engaged in activities that previously I have encountered only in library books. They arrange meetings in each other's houses by telephone, hold parties with conjurors who perform magic tricks, they ride, swim, play tennis, join the Girl Guides or Boy Scouts, go camping with rucksacks and tents. Their parents meet for meals, for drinks, for coffee, to play golf or bridge, or to arrange fund-raising events to help deprived children overseas. They lead, in other words, a perfectly ordinary mid-twentieth-century, middle-class existence.

My life at home and theirs seem to have little connection and I wonder and ponder on the discrepancies. Years later I realized that our worlds were anthropologically apart, that we came from different time-zones and different cultures; but by then it hardly mattered. I thought then, though, that there was a manifest physical difference. Certainly those children in Warrenpoint did not possess that placating look that we all had in those old photographs. Those children seemed shiny, as though the very process of being cared for had polished up their soft skin, buffed to shine by the lovely rub of affection. (Reading Tolstoy later I was amused and delighted to find his descriptions of a loved and cared-for and well-satisfied prince – 'He looked as fresh as a big glossy green Dutch cucumber.')

Looking at our old photographs I know now that we too were shiny; but I thought then that we were rickety, our bones joined carelessly, without grace, our skins thin and pallid. Many Catholic children then did look undernourished; and Protestant children, I believed, never looked anything other than cucumber-glossy. It was only when I went to Belfast, and saw in the traditionally Protestant areas children playing who had the same narrow limbs and white faces which I associated with the children of my own faith that I realized these were the physical marks and characteristics of the poor.

Later still, when living in New York in the late 1960s, I read of the fluttering astonishment and dismay among sociologists when they discovered the low self-image black children had of themselves and of each other, revealed to observers by the distorted, spidery self-portraits traced tentatively along the bottom of the page. When the same children were asked to draw white people, they drew large colourful portraits, centred on the page. No one who had been a member of an oppressed minority would have felt any surprise at those results.

Warrenpoint was then, and may still be, a segregated town. In the big houses along the sea-front, in the tree-lined streets, around the handsome square, lived the Protestants who ran the businesses and composed the professional classes. The golf club outside the town was exclusively Protestant. The Catholics lived in the back streets near the railway sidings, and when I went to Mass at the Catholic church I was always amazed at how many Catholic children there were – the church was full to overcrowding yet I never met any elsewhere. Later I recognize those I kneel among at Mass, shabbily dressed, playing in the back streets and down by the sea, beyond the point where the series of jutting breakwaters, seaweed-encrusted and barnacled, come to an end, marking the boundary of the beach as a social meeting-place.

Those children play in an anarchistic way there, pushing each other into the water, shouting and screaming and making a disturbance. Many wear old knickers instead of swimsuits. I lean over the high promenade wall and stare down at them, both repelled and drawn, for I should be down there with them and not up here with the gentry. The children look up and seeing me begin to shout catcalls. I am thrilled at their courage, feel a traitor and see how clearly they could be labelled sluts and outsiders; I am like a quadroon who in earlier days and other eras, hoping to pass for white, might shudder at a black person. It is a self-protective gesture.

In Warrenpoint too I commit the first mortal sin. It happens when I am with one of those shiny girls, the one who is my accredited official friend, and who is as suspicious of me as I am of her. Walking back from Alexander the baker's where they sell individual meringues, she bites into one and asks, 'Are you a Roman?' I do not know the term but I know instantly what she means. One moment I am pondering on the mystery of meringues – what they can possibly be made of, this crispy white exotic stuff so redolent of Warrenpoint, and how is the word spelt – the next a question has been asked to change my world. 'Are you?' she persists.

I know I must confess to being a Catholic, but I long to be accepted, to be like her, conforming, confident; and I know that she is that safe thing, a member of the Church of Ireland. I shake my head. 'What are you then?' There is a silence. 'Methodist', I say, inspired, and wait to be struck down. Nothing happens. She looks doubtful but cannot gainsay me. The meringue turns to ashes in my mouth and I go back to my aunt's house with a heavy heart, thinking of the gospel that has been read to us so often of how when Jesus had been arrested after his night in Gethsemane he had already prophesied that his friends would deny him, and how although Peter had been most vehement and angry in his denials, it was he who before the cock crowed twice had denied Him thrice.

I thought of the hymn I carolled so fervently at October Devotions: 'How sweet would be thy children's fate, if they, like them, could die for you. . . .' And I had thought as I sang of how I would have stood up straight and confessed my friendship, boasted of it. It is a bitter lesson to find I have denied Him under the quizzing of another girl. I think of the Christian martyrs, delivered to us daily in sermons and homilies as supreme examples of human endeavour, and the deaths they suffered, the endless mutilations described with such relish in our religion lessons and shown so graphically in the statues in the chapel. Lucy with her eyes torn out, Cecilia with her breasts cut off, Bartholomew displaying his flayed skin over his arm, Lawrence being grilled; and I know I can never join them in their maimed Heaven. All I can really think about is whether to confess to my aunt and see if she will back me up about being a Methodist. I incline to confessing – it's a habit, and I like the wonderful sticky glue that spreads through the veins after I have dumped the guilt.

'Do you remember that line of children?' I ask Eiram thirty years later.

'That was a most significant moment for me,' she says, her voice angry. 'I hate that memory passionately because I betrayed myself, and because of it I think I understand the thing of racial self-hatred, where a race turns in on itself, and feeds on the memories of inferiority, of others being superior. We hate ourselves both for letting it happen, for being inferior, and for allowing ourselves to become so. But how could we not? It's where the I.R.A. get part of their angry energy. We all know how you can demoralize an Irishman. Nobody is easier to demoralize by parading manners and social graces, and by making him feel socially ill at ease. That way you can make almost any Irish person feel uneasy or inferior. But touch him, lay a finger on him and he'll kill you. And somewhere now that is my own reaction. People can demoralize me. But let them violate me physically, show even a hint of aggression and I'm at their throats. It's a reaction from the gut. Oh, I remember that scene so well. Their bus was parked upon the New Road – and we had never seen a bus down there before, the roads were too narrow for buses. That rector in his grey suit. When they arrived where we were playing, and had always played, they spread themselves out and we shied away apologetically. We, who had spent all the days of our living memory on that shore, crept off.

'But why blame them? Blame ourselves, blame our upbringing, blame our religion, blame most of all our history. But I *do* blame them. We went further along the lough shore and went on playing and paddling and one girl followed us, pursued us. She said: "C'mere you two, are you two papishes?" I knew there was something amiss, and so did you, but I tried to answer the question, I said, "What are papishes? Papishes?" "You're papishes," she said. "Come on over here."

'We were scared, but her companions were with her, watching us, waiting, and we went over to her. She said "Say the Lord's Prayer. Go on say it, at once."

' "Our Father Who art in Heaven," I said. But you wouldn't say it. You wouldn't. You stood your ground. But I did, and when she heard "Who art in Heaven" instead of "which art" which is how they said it, she said, "You dirty wee papishes, you wee bitches, get on home." And we ran home crying, and said to Daddy, "What are papishes Daddy? They called us papishes."

'He was murderous. He got up and began to walk around the room, agitated. He knew we'd been defiled, and he's always been, you see, so unprejudiced, so unbigoted. I remember me saying to him about Wilbur who never went to Mass, "Daddy, Wilbur is he a Catholic or Protestant?" and him replying, "Eiram, what does it matter? It doesn't make a bit of odds." '

The thing that any outsider witnessing or listening to this story might find curious is how those children knew with such certainty, on the instant, that we were Catholics. We felt then that it was because of our appearance. But we know now that it had to do with language and words, still so potent in Ireland; and in so small a difference as Catholics using the form 'Our Father Who art in Heaven' and Protestants the form 'which art' lies a vast division. The very pronouns in speech are used to widen gaps between people who have nothing different about them but whose common history has made them enemies.

Almost every sentence we speak contains a word or expression, a twist or a phrase, a rearrangement of order, an irony or a bitterness which gives our speech great potency. The number of violent words, flashing angry imagery, and grotesque threats used in everyday speech reflects our history and condition. The strength of the oath, the fear of the curse, the belief in the efficacy of the prayer, the respect for words, for poetry, the quickness of wit, the flashing repartee, the fast outpourings of scorn – this verbal facility so characteristic of the Irish is bred deeply into us and the people around us. For when oral communication carries a whole heritage and becomes the only way to bequeath a culture to your descendants, then it must needs become the art of a nation. In secret Ireland the spoken and sung word has had to carry everything that painting, sculpture, scores, books, libraries, the museums and acknowledged repositories, the fruits of centuries of encouraged and open culture, carry in other countries.

The words we use are important. Our antique daily vocabulary seems to hang with more freight and meaning in each sentence than the pale nimble English we hear when we go out of the district to gentler or future places. We use a dialect studded with words and phrases that are either a literal translation from the Gaelic or are unchanged in pronunciation and usage since the enforced conversion of the Irish-speaking population to the English language.

The fear of the word, of humiliation and ridicule, is deeply inlaid in us, bred from the time when satire was the ultimate deterrent, used by bards as inescapable punishment and judgement against wrong-doers, especially those so powerful as to be inviolate from most other forms of violence. Certain words – amadan, kitterdy, tackle – are genuinely humiliating, and hoarded as though to preserve their venom. Their despatch through the air towards their target is laden and accurate. All the words to do with physical contact have a strange ambivalence. The word 'touch' is interchangeable with the word 'hit'. 'Don't touch her' means 'Don't beat or hit her,' never 'Don't caress her.' To dote on, which in ordinary English means you love someone, especially a baby, means in our vocabulary that you are wandering in your mind or are senile. And words more suitable for describing a hunt or to call down damnation are used almost casually in everyday speech. 'I'll slaughter you' is an ordinary threat from one of our teachers, and 'You'll go to hell if you do that' is a standard warning. Many an adult discovering some small offence will, as often as not, say 'I'll kill whoever did it,' and we in turn use these threats to each other as familiar utterances; in using them our voices take on a vehemence and passion that gives a dangerous edge to ordinary communications. Certain problems arise (which one might call overkill) – for how is authority to find more powerful deterrents, to preempt more serious offences, when you have been told you will be massacred for stepping in a puddle, or for not having done your homework?

When we leave Ireland we find that people are bemused or threatened or appalled by the passion and exaggeration in our speech. But such passion is a legacy of our history. The constant use of violent imagery and threat in the Irish version of the English language reflects the damage done to Ireland, and the ravages to the Irish spirit, through centuries in which the country and its people have suffered invasion, decimation, starvation, brutality and brutalization, contemptible legislation, eviction on a massive scale, emigration and religious persecution and savagery. If you mention memories and history as reasons for the language, outlook and behaviour of the Irish today, you are treated with contumely, as though you were trying to keep old hatreds alive by digging deep into some musty mausoleum for an obscure tract lost to human memory. But in the places where such things happened the memories are bitterly alive. We remember, for why should we forget. To forget is to stop lamenting those children whom Arthur Chichester saw in 1597 running naked across the burnt and scorched earth which his soldiers had devastated, towards the heat and warmth of the fire that had been lit expressly to lure them there for sport and slaughter.

Memory is re-enacted desire, and Ireland lives in the bones and flesh of her citizens. In that sense Ireland has no history, since the past is as real as the present and continues to happen and we all remain emotionally entwined with it in an apparently necessary conjunction of pain. The psychic violence done to the native Irish is so profound that the living perspective makes the history, rather than the actual old event. Incident after incident lives on in our memory. Here is one such, recorded by Isaac Butt:

On the estate of the Marquis of Lansdowne there lived, a few months ago, a man and his wife, Michael and Judith Donoghue; they lived in the house of one Casey. An order had gone forth on the estate (a common order in Ireland) that no tenant is to admit any lodger into his house. This was a general order. It appears, however, that sometimes special orders are given, having regard to particular individuals. The Donoghues had a nephew, one Denis Shea. The boy had no father living. He had lived with a grandmother who had been turned out of her holding for harbouring him. Denis Shea was twelve years old – a child of decidedly dishonest habits. Orders were given by the driver of this estate that this child should not be harboured upon it. This young Cain, thus branded and prosecuted, being a thief – he had stolen a shilling, a hen, and done many other such crimes as a neglected twelve-year-old famished child will do – wandered about. One night he came to his aunt Donoghue, who lodged with Casey. He had the hen with him.

Casey told his lodgers not to 'allow him in the house', as the agent's drivers had given orders about it. The woman, the child's aunt, took up a pike, or pitchfork, and struck him down with it; the child was crying at the time. The man, Donoghue, his uncle, with a cord tied the child's hands behind his back. The poor child after a while crawls or staggers to the door of one Sullivan, and tried to get in there. The maid of Sullivan called to Donoghue to take him away. This he did; but he afterwards returned with his hands still tied behind his back. Donoghue had already beaten him severely. The child seeks refuge in other cabins, but is pursued by his character – he was so bad a boy, the fear of the agent and the driver – all were forbidden to shelter him. He is brought back by some neighbours, in the middle of the night, to Casey's where his uncle and aunt lived. The said neighbours tried to force the sinking child in upon his relations. There is a struggle at the door. In the morning there is blood upon the threshold. The child is stiff dead – a corpse with its arms tied; around it every mark of a last fearful struggle for shelter, food, the common rights of humanity.

Irish history is littered with such charred emaciated corpses. Their

160

stoor still chokes us, and because of the continuity with the past we know intimately in the spring of our blood who those children were. They were the makings of each one of us, and that part of me which is still connected with their sufferings makes me want to turn on my rational present educated other part and rend myself in half, or tear one part from the other so that one part of me can wholly hate.

Self-esteem, that fragile and necessary attribute, is easily enough removed from vulnerable people and individuals of any tribe living under official contempt. In their subsequent loss of confidence they will turn on themselves, become fiercely protective, and yet find little that is lovable among or about themselves. Part of this bequest is the self-hatred and dolorousness that poisons so many of the lives around us. In seeking a means of escape from this coil some terrible injuries are self-inflicted, although a person who is scorched while escaping from a burning house can hardly be said to have inflicted his injuries on himself.

All children born in segregated places are born with a dark caul, a web of ambiguities around them, from which it is difficult to struggle free. But the Roman Catholic children of the province of Northern Ireland have a darker, stronger birth-membrane imprisoning them against which they have to struggle, since the loyalties and love we feel towards our putative nation and powerful religion are subversive. Loyalty towards the idea of Ireland and love for Mother Church are inextricably entangled, yet neither feeling can be open, proud or free, since neither religion nor country has status, official sanction or respect. The feelings we have or cultivate for these important influences in our lives are something akin to the love we feel for the women around us – protective, fierce, yet contemptuous, because they are not powerful, and not respected or even recognized by the powers that we know to be.

Northern Ireland for us is neither one thing nor the other; in it we are neither English nor Irish. We are taught English history as the record of our past, and whenever the history or culture of Ireland is mentioned it is presented as arcane, obscure, and unconnected with the country in which we live and the people to which we belong. We read English literature and recite English poetry without anyone making the point that many of the writers and poets we study have come from our country. We study natural history, but it is all done from reference books dealing with the English countryside. No reference is ever made to the lough, just beyond the school-yard, and its unique shoals of fish. At school we sing English folk songs, and warble *Greensleeves, Barbara Allen* and *Scarborough Fair*. At home my father sings *My Lagan Love* in his cracked and off-key voluptuous voice, but I never hear his song as a distinct expression of a nation's voice and memory.

From my earliest days I know I am a member of the national Irish family, and in the same way that I am linked by such strong blood-ties to my own family that my membership of it is taken for granted, that I move only within its stretch and shelter, I am also linked to Irish history; and my perceptions and awareness of our past brings that forgiving knowledge that members of a family have of each other, an awareness of early hidden reasons for behaviour which to the less affected or engaged observer might merely appear as aberrant, or unreasonable. Old issues and grievances that in other circumstances could and would have sunk into history are living and unrepentant in our history still. We are bequeathed this nervous interest and enmeshment in our past as our best inheritance, entrusted with it like a sacrament.

We are reminded at every turn of our oppression and are reinforced in an idea of our true native Irishness – not by our parents who are not at all fanatical, but by our neighbours, by the songs that are sung, by the words and expressions we use and by many of the young men who nurture a heavy rage against the oppressor – that is, anyone who is not a Catholic, from the local police sergeant to the Sovereign of England; and for these men and many Republicans of that period, the Catholic religion and patriotism are so linked they are as one.

The fact that many of the heroes of the 1916 Rising, the pinnacle of heroic achievement in their eyes, were Protestant or Anglo-Irish is ignored or disbelieved. The religious crusading aspects of the Republican cause, the sexist theology, the belief that the real Irishman can only be a hero ready to die for his country (and that country having always been symbolized as a female) seem to produce a pathologically masculine Irishman

162

whose idea of masculinity is a kind of disease connected with bloodshed, violence, valour. 'Bloodshed', wrote Padraic Pearse, one of the leaders of the 1916 rebellion, who indeed died for his adopted country, 'is a cleansing and a sanctifying thing and the nation which regards it as the final horror has lost its manhood.' The effective heroes of Ireland, the men who did so much in getting legislation passed to lighten the lot of the Irish, like Henry Grattan – whose famous assertion that 'the Irish Protestant could never be free till the Irish Catholic had ceased to be a slave' showed both camps how closely they were hoist – or Daniel O'Connell, whose courageous determination to avoid bloodshed is interpreted by many as demonstrating a final lack of courage and commitment to the cause of Irish nationalism, are not revered in the same way in public memory, are not what the Irish call 'real' heroes, heroes as national monuments.

These endless reminders of our past are not tendered to us as forms of atonement, or of ritual, but in order to keep the idea of a future revenge uppermost in our minds. Somewhere, those who speak so continuously of a United Ireland in this semi-religious way believe they can overturn the society in which they live without overturning themselves. Burke reflecting on the Revolution in France wrote: 'They should not think it amongst their rights to cut off the entail or commit waste on the inheritance by destroying at their pleasure the whole original fabric of their society, hazarding to leave to those who come after them a ruin instead of a habitation.'

In most of the houses up and down the road to the Cross there are relics and mementos of the 1916 Easter Rising in Dublin which began the war that eventually led to the founding of the Irish Free State. The Irish tricolour flag is more often than not tucked behind the framed text of the famous speech from the dock made by Robert Emmet who was executed for his part in a revolution in 1803 that was doomed to failure from the start. It is quoted to us so often we know it by heart:

I have but one request to ask at my departure from this world; it is the charity of its silence. Let no man write my epitaph; for as no man who knows my motives dare now indicate them, let not prejudice, nor ignorance asperse them. Let them and me rest in obscurity and peace; and my tomb remain uninscribed and my memory in oblivion, until other times and other men can do justice to my character. When my country takes her place among the nations of the earth then, and not till then, let my epitaph be written.

It was a speech that inspired the people of Ireland when it was first uttered extempore at his trial, and it continues to inspire – although by this time it is as much an inspiration towards hatred as towards the fulfilment of the ideal that Emmet died for. 'I acted as an Irishman', he said, 'determined on delivering my country from the yoke of a foreign and unrelenting tyranny and the more galling yoke of a domestic faction which is its joint-partner and perpetrator in the patricide. . . .'

There is a feeling of anger and resentment underlying the apparently calm political exterior of our parish, an anger kept alive and bubbling by the system of discrimination that drifts like spore from Stormont, the seat of government where the Unionist Party is in power. It is an organized official system of discrimination built into the state of Northern Ireland, from its very inception, and any attempts to remedy the situation are met by fierce opposition and venomous provocation from the establishment and political leaders at every level, all of whom are members of the Orange Order. Indeed this secret Order and the Unionist Party are inextricably linked, and it is virtually impossible to rise in the Unionist Party without being a member of the Orange Order.

Called Orange to commemorate the victory of King William of Orange (whom Ulster Loyalists supported) over James II (the Catholic contender) at the Battle of the Boyne, its members are a powerful freemasonry dedicated to helping each other, to continuing the exclusion of Catholics from any passage to power, and to keeping partisan issues alive. 'In times of tension', wrote Charles Brett, an eminent Belfast leader and lawyer, in his book about Northern Ireland, *Long Shadows Cast Before*, published in 1978, 'the Orange Order becomes a secret society, not merely, as its members claim, a society with secrets; it acts as a focus for bigotry and extremism; it invites onto its platforms and to the pulpits at its religious services, only those Protestant clergy who can be trusted to be outspoken in their hostility to Rome. The connection between Orangeism and the Protestant paramilitary armies of the present day is unproven; it is probably untrue that a majority of Orangemen are paramilitaries; but I suspect it to be true that a majority of Protestant paramilitaries are Orangemen.'

Soon after the State of Northern Ireland was founded the then spokesman for the Unionist Party, Sir George Clark, said: 'I would draw your attention to the words civil and religious liberty. This liberty we know is the liberty of the Protestant religion.' And these attitudes had not changed much among the establishment in the intervening years. Discrimination was manifested in almost everything; it was part of the hierarchy, the job-structure, the social services, in the continuum of the political life of the province. We met with discrimination in everyday life and we know we will meet it in the limits to our future; and our parents have to live in an irresponsible democracy based on the system of gerrymandering. The basic ploy of the gerrymander is to draw constituency or ward boundaries so as to spread the desired support over as many seats as possible and crowd opponents into as few as possible. In most constituencies with Catholic majorities boundaries were drawn so that two Unionist M.P.s could be returned with narrow majorities for one massively supported non-Unionist M.P.

The system of representation means that for the twenty years between 1943 and 1963 so overwhelmingly Unionist was the establishment that there was no Catholic in the Northern Ireland cabinet; Lord Brookeborough, who during these years was Prime Minister of Northern Ireland, boasted that he would never employ a Catholic on his staff, and that he had never crossed into the Republic of Ireland. In 1971, Terry Coleman recorded in an interview this remarkable statement from a man who was head of a state in which there were over half a million Catholics in a population of over one million people:

'You see this argument that's going on why don't you have Roman Catholics in your cabinet, well to me that would be exactly like the British Government during the last war having a German in the Admiralty and a German in the War Office.'

But surely, Coleman ventured, surely he would not go so far

as to call Roman Catholics traitors? 'Well, needn't use the word traitor I suppose.'

In 1971 when Brookeborough was asked in a newspaper interview about gerrymandering, he said, 'I really don't know that one. I never came up against it.'

The journalist Harold Jackson, writing about Brookeborough's long administration, concluded: 'The iron rule of Lord Brookeborough ensured that a surface tranquillity pervaded and no one in Westminster felt inclined to poke a stick into the mess bubbling underneath.' The more militant among the Catholic population did, however, and the Irish Republican Army, an illegal underground organization, tried to stir the mess by launching in 1956 a campaign of guerilla activities against the state. They hoped to galvanize the Catholic population into beginning a definitive struggle, but the vast majority of Catholics preferred to live under a system of injustices so long as it was tolerable; and it was only when the intolerance became intolerable and the grievances unbearable that enough Catholics finally felt impelled to try to change things. Analysing what had happened, the lawyer Charles Brett wrote: 'I think the Unionists could, without the slightest risk to their entrenched positions of power, have met these Catholic grievances with a spirit of fairness and generosity. Had they done so, I do not believe that any of the Troubles of the years since 1969 need have occurred.'

Years and years after that revelation on the lough shore I sat beside Lord Brookeborough at a dinner party. I was alarmed and rather flattered to find myself next to him. I was young, and uneasy. I was there because I was writing a story for a magazine, and so I already felt in the position of a governess – neither with the servants, nor with the guests, but posed uneasily between the two. It is perhaps to my hostess's credit that she put me beside the guest of honour, regardless of my ambivalent position. She may only have seen a *placement* that needed to be done and imagined, I suppose, that any young woman eager to please and ready to sing for her supper would make an agreeable dinner companion for the old man.

The dinner progressed. He treated me with a heavy-handed flirtatiousness. I tried to regard him objectively, this man who personalized bigotry for me, who by his actions and attitudes had exacerbated the divisions in the community of which he was the leader, and who had contributed to the ruination of many of my contemporaries' lives.

At the end of the meal he said: 'Tell me – I didn't quite hear your name . . . ?'

'Devlin,' I said, looking at him; and seeing his face shiver and pinch inwards I said again more clearly, 'Devlin.'

I might have hit him across the face. The name could only be that of a Catholic. His long head swivelled away, his hooded eyes grew more blinkered.

'Devlin,' he said and fell silent. And then he turned back. He said, 'You've come far.' And turned away, nor spoke to me again that evening. I sat winded, my anger bubbling under my stricken heart. I had betrayed myself, but what was I to do? I hadn't come far enough if I had arrived at a seat beside him. Sitting at that table a scene came into my mind, erupted into it, perfect, sudden, like a shaken scene in a crystal ball.

We have been out with our father for a drive in the old Austin to visit Coalisland where Ellen lives, and where the pots and crocks we use in our dairy are made in a small pottery, and thence we have driven towards Dungannon. It is a hot July day and the car windows are open and as we get near the town an extraordinary noise comes rolling down the hill and buries us in a throbbing, pounding rhythm, erotic in its beating intensity. As the astounding and primaeval noise cascades down through the air over us I know the message it is pounding out is directed against *us*. But what have we done? My father stops the car and says quietly, 'There are some bad boys up there.'

It is my first real experience of the dramatic and coarse expression of religious intolerance which is so much to the taste of the people of Ulster; but it is only now sitting beside Brookeborough that I can reciprocate the hatred that those men, beating their drums in their black tattoo on that July morning years before, feel towards us. I can taste it, the voluptuous hatred bubbling down in my veins, a rich seething mixture of anger and frustration, spite and impotence, a rage that I didn't know I had, a hatred

167

that is like a plague, a plague that my parents with their care and liberalism had tried to inoculate us from, but which too many others had already caught for us to escape infection. As I sit silent and isolated at that table I become for myself a parable for the situation of all of us Catholics in Ulster. I remember the hill and the noise, and it is too painful to bear and I leave the table.

16

There was, at the end, nothing dramatic about our leaving and our parting. Time came along; not between us, because even its dreadfully fast passage could never disturb that fixed eternity between us, the setting of time in which each of us is placed in the family ring; but it carried us on and out to the world that was waiting.

For us, where we grew up was as much a place of the mind as a place in itself, and like the children in the fairy story we dropped a secret marking-trail or wound an invisible thread so that we could always find our way back. 'I don't think that we can any of us ever get free even if we wanted to,' Sinclare said once, 'and that's partly because we lived in such a paradoxical way there, completely rooted in a powerful place, and yet knowing that we had to tear and claw at those roots and leave it to get anywhere else, to have our future.'

I always wanted my childhood to be like the wood I buried along the shore so that it would remain, petrifying, enduring, while I hurried ahead to find out how to live it. But I could never find the buried wood, no matter how I looked for it. I never knew where to return, and I never knew when, and I never knew where to look for that lost childhood until my sisters, grown up but still connected, showed me how and where; and Eiram's husband Seamus showed me in his incomparable poetry that the place I dreamed of was authentic.

When I go home I still walk that same stretch of road to the shore. It is remarkably unchanged. The old men who lean on their gates waiting and watching children with the same endless curiosity for my approach and that of my daughters are sons grown into the silhouette of their fathers. Some of them have been on holiday to the United States, visiting the brothers and sisters who emigrated so painfully fifty years ago on an irrevocable voyage that they never could have imagined would one day become a matter for holiday and frivolity for those they left so sorrowfully behind. The men appear unchanged, unmarked by their transatlantic adventures. Perhaps the place they live in has marked them, as it has me, in a way no younger place can ever disturb.

The same wild rose, appearing as the most useless, fragile and ephemeral thing of all in that necessary landscape, is still entwined with the hawthorn and the sloe in the hedges outside what once was Feley Cassidy's house, although his garden and little orchard which had the best apples in the district have been ripped out and ploughed under, and the strangely proportioned house that always looked as though most of it had slithered underground, and in which he and his brother Johnny and sister Lena wrangled and bickered, scrambled and wrought throughout their lives, is mouldering and agape.

The little shed built of square stone from the lough shore, of various shades of grey and slate ranging from the colour of the breast of a dove almost to an indigo blue, making the shed look like a vivid cubist painting, has tumbled, disregarded as an artefact, without value, although such buildings can never be recreated. The same number of the same indeterminate breed of feral dog still lie in the middle of the road at the opening of the loanings. And a dog like the Dallys' lunges at our ankles, but the old silent Dally brothers are all dead and their house has vanished: not even the mound remains. A bungalow stands on the site, and I know it is a lot easier to live in than the old two-roomed cottage.

The Cross, the ancient Celtic monument looming above the water that bolts our district on to the lough shore, and bolts it too into the imagination and lore and knowledge of many people who have never seen it, remains the same; but the graveyard surrounding it is tidied up and levelled out, and the Pin Tree has gone, finally killed with copper poisoning. Even its roots have been levered out, and now the graves extend into every corner of the graveyard; there are no visible circles where older dispensations still hold sway.

But these uneasy changes seem small. The changes along the lough shore just below are bigger, more brutal and more violating.

The sally trees on which the fishermen hung their nets to dry, like gargantuan spider-webs glimmering in the dawn, no longer stand among the whin-bushes and wild iris along the shore of the lough; those trees and the bushes have vanished under the ambitious wheels of a tractor belonging to the farmer who bought Lizzie Treanor's shaggy farm and ancient shoreland after she had died coughing, defiant to the end. He has transformed that lovely sedgy boulder-strewn marshland to a flat productive arable field, although I can still discern the old wavering shoreline below this neatly hemmed one. I mourn the old stony humpy shore, much as I used to mourn what I thought was my own lost landscape.

The air is leached of colour and the lough of its proper edge. I sit on the gravestone and look towards Golloman's Point with its grove of sally trees, and Gusty's lights shimmering behind them up in that remote wooded area lying locked so intimately into the lough, linked only to the New Road by the rampar where the stone bearing the hoof-print of the stolen cow had lain until it too was stolen. To the right is Durrish's house, to which the people had come for a cure; when we lay on the walls of the church, it had been so surrounded by trees and hedges that only its chimney was visible. Now it stands bleak and shorn and visibly empty.

I sit on the gravelly stone and stare at the lough's waters remembering the melodramas that were daily played out on its surface when I believed that a city lay beneath its waves and that it claimed a life every year. In our father's public house the fishermen had sung a melancholy dirge about it:

On Lough Neagh's banks, where the fisherman strays
On a cool clear evening declining
You can see the round towers of other days,
In the waves beneath them shining
Thus shall memory often in days gone by

Catch a glimpse of the days that are over
And silently mourn for the times gone by
And the long buried glories they cover.

Now we are growing old; I cannot believe it; to me we are all always among the kingdom of the young. 'The past is the only dead thing that smells sweet,' wrote Edward Thomas; and when I first read that, fighting to get free, I thought that was why I was so connected with the past, why I wanted to remain buried in it. But I realize now that the past is alive, like all Irish history.

Watching my sisters with their children, I know I am still linked to those sisters in my inner life as in my outer one, as linked to them as the children they were, through my mind and psyche, as I am to my own children in my daily life. My relationships with my daughters are simulacra of those I have had with my sisters – extreme, loving, jealous, harsh, and I imagine bewildering to them, since they are, after all, new people and sisters to themselves. Bewildering too to me, since I do not always recognize what I am trying to do, to call back yesterday to bring back those I fear I have lost, my long-gone darlings.

I want terribly to be free of them, I suppose, but those childhood apprehensions still carry a warning that if I free myself of them, if I let them go, they will vanish, and I shall be alone. Even worse, I fear that if I banish them or let them slip out of my frantic memory or grasp, I shall annihilate them; that, as they slide down the rope of memory and out of my view, they might cease to exist and these powerful phantoms of my imagination will be murdered by my ceasing to remember them.

I do not need to be told, I think, that as a child I may have wanted them all to die, to leave me alone. I hold on to their fictive life the harder to avert the calamity of my own loss. I have other fears and motives too. Somewhere I believe that as long as they haunt me I can hope for the ultimate last impossible consolation: the restoration of innocence.

I walk back from the Cross in the dusk, up to the Cross roads, past where the gate to that Ultima Thule created by my father lies hidden, past the ruins of Biddy's house and the filled-in well, its spring no longer needed. I am no longer afraid of banshees and black dogs and the living dead, and I look up the loanings to the houses where the neighbours congregated for the evening's crack, and where the soft blur of oil-lamps lit one single window in every house. I see pouring out of the new windows the flickering ghastly light of the television, as though a luminous ectoplasmic plague has entered every house spreading a virulent international infection, destroying the recipe for being a community; a ghostly flame searing the matted fabric of that way of life woven so carefully through so many lives in so many generations, and leaving for our children only scorched earth where once there was the luxuriant vegetation of living tradition.

If I close my eyes I can smell my childhood, I can feel the crackle of Elizabeth's blue taffeta dress with the big collar edged with white stars, hear Ellen calling the men in for the tea, her voice making the horses stamp and whinny, see my father lying with his raven head on his propped hand finishing a line of poetry.

The horses that stamped their enormous feet and jangled their harness and brasses in the high summer days of our childhood are dead. The brasses are curios on someone's shelf, the greath has disintegrated; the meadows are rushy; the keshes over which Tamsie negotiated are bridged by nothing but rotting holed planks, the corncrake is extinct. Francey MacAllister is an alcoholic and beats his children, and the pink corrugated shed with its arched roof is echoing; although the sun still pours through the holes at the top, it falls through emptiness to stones at the bottom. I try to bring my sisters out of the shadows of our mutual past and into the light of my memory, to make them shine at the point of my pen. But they will not stay together, they are away on down behind the hayshed, or lying in the fork of the copper beech or staring up at the leaves of the enormous rhubarb plants or pressing frightened against a wall. They cannot be transported into my ken, cannot be moved to where I want them.

I want to cry, to feel again the impotent despair of childhood; and then I look again and see that they are all in their own places, leading their own rich lives, and that they love me. I stop calling and calling, for I hear for the first time their voices calling back and I know at last, but for the first time, that I can never be lost since my sisters will always know, as they always have known, where I am, and will find me.